REBECCA
A WOMAN
OF FAITH

GEORGIA JACKSON

TEACH Services, Inc.
PUBLISHING
www.TEACHServices.com • (800) 367-1844

World rights reserved. This book or any portion thereof may not be copied or reproduced in any form or manner whatever, except as provided by law, without the written permission of the publisher, except by a reviewer who may quote brief passages in a review.

The author assumes full responsibility for the accuracy of all facts and quotations as cited in this book. The opinions expressed in this book are the author's personal views and interpretations, and do not necessarily reflect those of the publisher.

This book is provided with the understanding that the publisher is not engaged in giving spiritual, legal, medical, or other professional advice. If authoritative advice is needed, the reader should seek the counsel of a competent professional.

Copyright © 2025 Georgia Jackson

Copyright © 2025 TEACH Services, Inc.

ISBN-13: 978-1-4796-1748-7 (Paperback)

ISBN-13: 978-1-4796-1749-4 (ePub)

Library of Congress Control Number: 2024916551

All scripture quotations are taken from King James Version. Public domain.

Published by

TABLE OF CONTENTS

The Encounter	5
The Early Years	9
The Madrid Years	15
The Kingman Years	19
The Albuquerque and Las Vegas Years	23
The Teaching Years	27
The Early Married Years	33
The War Years	41
Return to Albuquerque	55
The 1950s	73
The 1960s	85
The Weatherford Years	97
The Lonely Years	109
Her Years with Me	121
Conclusion	139

THE ENCOUNTER

As they walked out of the school gymnasium, Emily turned to her sister, Rebecca, and asked, "What did you think of that?"

"Well, I don't know. I've never heard anything like that before. I was always taught that Sunday is the Sabbath, the Lord's Day. Have you ever heard anything like this before?" Rebecca was not impulsive and when exposed to a new idea, she took time to think it through before making up her mind to accept or reject it.

"Yes, I have," Emily replied, "While I was in Montana, with Daddy, I borrowed a book from the next-door neighbor, called *The Marked Bible*. It's the story of a young man who was raised a Christian. To keep from going to prison, he joined the Merchant Marines, and when he left home, his mother gave him a Bible she had marked. He was so angry at her and the world, he just threw it overboard. Later, on one of his trips, he served with a Christian captain, and they had some missionaries on board who worshiped on Saturday and showed from the Bible that the Sabbath is Saturday. Before I had a chance to finish it, Mary [their other sister] grabbed it out of my hands, marched over to the neighbor lady and told her to keep her filthy literature home, that we weren't interested in it. So, I never had a chance to finish it." (Won't this dear sister be surprised when she gets to heaven and discovers that her lending that book resulted in the conversation between those two?)

Behind them a soft, male voice spoke. "I have that book at home. If you want, I'll bring it tomorrow night." The two girls turned to see who had spoken and saw young Mr. Will Fisher, the son of one of the prominent families standing there.

"I would really appreciate it," Emily said. "I do want to finish the book; it was very interesting."

The time was August 1934. My mother, Rebecca King, was there, preparing to teach school that year, and her youngest sister, Emily, was visiting with her before going to Albuquerque to start attending high school. This was during the great depression, so anything that could be considered entertainment and was free was well attended.

The place was the little town of Stanley, east of Albuquerque, New Mexico. The year before, a Baptist evangelist had held a tent revival there and had raised up a little church. But, being an evangelist, he had moved on. Mrs. Fisher, after thinking over the situation, was sure that without some kind of leadership, the group would just disband and sink back into their old ways. She suggested that they meet for prayer meeting each week in her home, as there was no church building. Within the next year, they had all studied the Bible, learned about the prophecies in Daniel and Revelation, and had accepted the seventh-day Sabbath as taught in the Bible. At the end of that time, she had written to the Texico Conference and told them they were ready to form a small company. About the same time, another small group of Adventists, who lived south of there, had written to the conference stating that they had some young people who needed to be baptized. Their response was to send out an evangelist to hold ten meetings. Mother always said there were five meetings, but the records at the conference office show that there were ten. Obviously, since Mother and Aunt Emily had just arrived in town, they weren't aware of the five that had been held the previous week.

The next night, Will Fisher brought the book, and Emily very happily took it home and finished reading it that night. Rebecca picked it up and started reading it the next day. At first, she just read it, enjoying the story, but when it started giving Bible texts, she realized there was more there than just a story, so she started reading it again and looked up every Bible text as it was given. When she finished the book, she was convinced that the seventh day was the true Sabbath. She didn't know or understand any of the other doctrines and really shouldn't have been baptized. I'm sure on the proceeding nights the pastor had covered such things as Christ's second coming and baptism, but since they weren't there, they had missed those lessons.

At the end of the meetings, they had a baptism for those who hadn't been baptized the previous summer. In fact, Rebecca argued with the pastor that her baptism in the Episcopalian church was as good as the others who were joining by profession of faith. He firmly stated that if she wanted to join them, she had to be immersed. She finally agreed. This included the young people from the other group, Rebecca, Emily, and another man who lived in the area. If Mother ever told me his name, I don't remember it, and the records don't give any names, just that eight people joined the church.

Mrs. Fisher and the evangelist talked to Aunt Emily about going to attend the academy at Southwestern Junior College (SWJC), in Keene, Texas, and when Mother said that she would help pay for it, she agreed to go. She was there that year, then lived with a family for two years, I think, teaching their children. She went back to SWJC at a later date to get more schooling. Mother said that when Aunt Emily went to registrar the second time, she was asked if she owed for her other year's schooling. "I'm afraid I do," Aunt Emily said, so the lady went to look up her records.

When she returned, she said, "Yes, you do. You owe seventy-five cents," which Aunt Emily happily paid. At some time during the preceding years, she was married, but if I ever heard the name of the man she married, I don't remember it. The marriage only lasted a short time, probably because she was still very young and not wise enough to select a man who would treat her as he should.

Anyway, a Sabbath School class was organized after their baptism, and Mother attended it while teaching that school year. She had married my father the preceding May, but they hadn't announced their marriage because the state wasn't hiring married teachers, and Mother wanted to teach that year. Daddy got a job driving the school bus and did some other odd jobs around town until that spring. That was when he arranged to farm a little place out of town. They were married again that following October in Las Lunas, New Mexico.

Mrs. Fisher had known Mother before this, since Mother had taught her children

> *She was very aware that Mother had not been ready for baptism. Her solution was to give Mother the Conflict of the Ages books. When Mother had finished reading them, she was a true believer and understood what the Bible taught about our beliefs.*

one other year. She was very aware that Mother had not been ready for baptism. Her solution was to give Mother the *Conflict of the Ages* books. When Mother had finished reading them, she was a true believer and understood what the Bible taught about our beliefs. She also studied the Sabbath School lesson daily and that helped.

At the end of the school year, she joined my father on the little place where he was farming, and they never lived in town again, until World War II started. I think it was the second spring that Daddy found the place where we lived until he went into the Marine Corps in 1942. There wasn't a church closer than Stanley, too far for Mother to go, so she kept the Sabbath at home, and after we children arrived, she taught us to keep the Sabbath with her. She subscribed to the *Review & Herald*, *Signs of the Times*, and *Youth's Instructor*. After we were born, she subscribed to *The Little Friend* for us. We diligently kept the Sabbath, but since there was no church near, we were unable to attend and therefore didn't know how to behave in church. More on this later.

THE EARLY YEARS

She was born to John Kenneth and Leona Wells King on May 31, 1909, at her grandmother's house in Missouri. Since Granddad worked for the railroad, he had free passes and sent Grandmother to be with her mother for the birth of their first child, which was my mother. She was named for her two aunts, Nina, her mother's sister, and Rebecca, for her father's sister. Mother was always called Rebecca, never Becky. In later life, she dropped the name Nina, and even some of the family members didn't know that it was her first name.

Mother's parents had met at Liberal, Kansas, where Leona's aunt ran the Harvey House, the old motel/cafe for the railroad men. From what I understand, she was rather wild, and her aunt was afraid she would get into trouble, so she engineered the marriage. John and Leona certainly never talked before their marriage, and there was never any real love between them. Every one of their children talked about the terrible verbal fights they had, but it never got physical. They separated when Aunt Emily, the youngest, was about six, I think. I do know that every one of them made it plain to their spouse before marriage that they would never fight in front of the children. My parents certainly never did.

They had five children: Mother, John, Mary, Bill, and Emily. Granddad said he wanted six, but the doctor said that Grandmother shouldn't have any more, and he didn't insist. I'm not sure when they moved to Canada, but I do know that Mary was born there. Granddad was working on the Grand Trunk Railroad; it was being built at that time. He managed to find a boxcar and made it into a "trailer house" for them. He papered the inside with construction paper and put in a wood burning stove to heat it. It was a real improvement on what the other people (mostly men) had; they lived in tents or wood shacks. When they needed to move, as the line was built, he hitched it to one of the engines and moved it along. The food was cooked at a central kitchen, so Grandmother didn't have to do any cooking, but, at mealtime, she would sometimes send Mother, who was five, and Uncle John, who was three, to get the food. Mother said that one time their father saw them with the pans on their heads going for the food, and he sent them home to have the pans washed before returning for the food.

Back then, Granddad would get up early, light the stove, dress, and go to work. Grandmother would stay in bed with the children until the boxcar was warm. I suppose she usually went back to sleep. This incident happened when Aunt Mary was about ten months old, so it was probably in October or November. It had already snowed, so it was very cold outside. As usual, Granddad had lit the fire and gone to work. When Grandmother awoke, the whole end of the boxcar was on fire.

The stove pipe was hot, and the construction paper had come loose and touched the red-hot pipe, causing it to blaze. My grandmother could never think in an emergency. She jumped out of bed, threw on her coat, and ran outside and down the track looking for help, but no one was very close. Meanwhile, there were three small children in that blazing boxcar. When Grandmother did find someone, his first thoughts were for the children, so he rushed back and found that my mother—young as she was at the time—had gotten little John and baby Mary outside. The children were sitting on a snowbank, wrapped in a quilt.

It didn't take long for others to arrive, and they started pouring water on the outside of the boxcar, which did no good. Shortly after that Granddad arrived, grabbed two buckets of water, went to the door, threw one bucket of water one way and the other the opposite way and essentially put out the fire. Since the boxcar was of heavy timber, it wasn't badly damaged. However, they lost everything they had. Grandmother was in her nightgown and coat; the children in their night clothes had one quilt. Fortunately, the company had a store where the people could get clothes—for men—so Grandmother had to wear men's clothing until they could get an order off to Montgomery Ward. I'm not sure how they clothed the children until the order came in. The company was very good to them. Grandmother said that they had already started to build them a cabin before Granddad got there, so they would have some shelter that night.

I think it was while they were in Canada that Mother had her most memorable Christmas, at least the one she talked about the most. They had gone to a church for the gathering on Christmas Eve. She said it was full of people, and there was a very large tree (for a small child any tree is very large), and it was covered with things, toys of every kind. One thing that caught her eye was a beautiful doll. They were sitting next to another family that had a small girl, probably about the same age as Mother. From the first, the little girl loudly proclaimed that the doll was going to be hers. It was one of the last things taken from the tree. Apparently, when each thing was taken down, the name of the person for whom it was intended was called out, and the person went to the front to receive it. When the doll was taken down, Mother's name was called. She was really surprised, thinking the doll was for the other little girl. Granddad pushed her forward, and she reluctantly went and got it. The other little girl was crying, and Mother wanted to give it to her, thinking that it really was for her, but Granddad wouldn't let her. It made a very deep impression on Mother; she never forgot it.

Granddad would have stayed with that railroad, but when World War One started, everything shut down, so he sent Grandmother and the children back to the States to stay with his parents until he got there. Since they were essentially in the wilderness, there was nowhere to spend his good salary. They had quite a bit of money saved, probably around a thousand dollars.

Naturally, he sent that money with her. On the trip home, she left her purse on the seat while going into the dining car. Two men opened it, found the money, and took it. They made a stop at Platt City, Kansas, where her two boy cousins met her. She told them that her money had been stolen, and she pointed out the two men who had taken it. They accosted the two men, but when asked how much she had, she didn't know and gave a small figure, if I remember right, about two hundred dollars. The men returned what she asked for. Her cousins thought she probably had much more, but they couldn't make the men give any more, so that was what she arrived with at her in-law's house. Granddad arrived, expecting to have enough money to last until he could get another job, only to find that they were practically broke. He got a job harvesting the wheat, but then his mother discovered that Grandmother was pregnant again and told them to get out.

Granddad contacted an old friend who owned a cattle ranch in the panhandle of Texas, so they moved there, and they were there until they moved to Clovis, New Mexico, when Mother was eight, so she and Uncle John could go to school. There was no school close, so the other women taught their children, but Grandmother refused to do that, even though Granddad bought the books she would need. Grandmother hated the ranch and everything about it. She had been raised on a farm in Missouri, and when she left there, she vowed she would never live on a farm (or ranch) again. And, other than that time, she never did.

While they lived on the ranch, an incident occurred that both Mother and Aunt Mary told me about. It probably happened not too long before they moved to Clovis, since Aunt Mary remembered it. They used wood for their heating and cooking, so Granddad took a wagon and the family down to an arroyo to get supplies. One of the things he did while there was to give each child a wad of "gum." This was the pinon sap that had dried, so it had to be chewed and the hard-shell spit out. While he was cutting down the trees, he was chewing and spitting, so each child could have a wad. Probably getting enough wood took most of the day, and it was a pleasant time for all. When the wagon was full of wood, they started home. In getting up the side of the arroyo, the wagon overturned. All but Aunt Mary were either thrown out or not in the wagon, but when all the dust had settled, they saw that no one was hurt except Aunt Mary, who was under the wood, and they could hear her crying. Grandmother, as usual, became hysterical, and Granddad started throwing wood off the top of her. Grandmother started crying, saying over and over again, "She's dead! She's dead!"

Granddad's answer was short, as he was throwing logs, "She's not dead. If she were, she wouldn't be crying." When she was uncovered, they discovered that she wasn't hurt either. She had simply lost her gum, and that was the reason for her tears.

Granddad worked for the water department in Clovis for about two years, I think, then started working in the mines as an electrician. That was a very unsettled time for them. Granddad was moving frequently, so he sent Mother and Uncle John to stay with his parents in Wynnewood, Oklahoma that year. Fortunately, his sister, Rebecca, was there, and she took care of them. Mother never talked about it until later when her mind wasn't good. She told me that her grandmother would hardly speak to them. Their Aunt Sylvia (Granddad's sister, who had "cheated" him out of an education—more on that later) was there with her children, and they were welcomed with joyful, open arms, which really distressed Mother.

According to Mother, her grandmother King never liked her mother, but as she said, "She wouldn't have liked anyone Daddy married." Before his marriage, Granddad always earned a good salary, but he was very frugal. He took out what little he needed and sent the rest to his parents. His mother looked upon his wife as depriving them of his wages.

On the other hand, their Grandmother Wells, their maternal grandmother, was very good to them. From what I understand, they saw very little of her, but she sent them packages every few months full of things she had knitted or crocheted for them. She kept them in mittens, socks, caps, and such. She also cut the funnies out of her newspaper and included them, which was a pure delight to the children. She was much loved by all five of them. When I was pregnant with my oldest daughter, she sent all of us, Mother, Aunt Mary, Aunt Monnie (Bill's wife), and both of my sisters and me, handbags she had crocheted for us. I still have mine—one of the few things I have managed to hang on to through the years.

THE MADRID YEARS

The next year, they lived in Madrid (pronounced, at least by Granddad, MAD-rid), New Mexico, and they were there for the next three years. From what Mother said, those were happy years for her and the other children. Granddad's brother, Uncle Tommy, lived with them at least part of the time, and he had an old camera. Mother enjoyed taking pictures and had an album of them from that time. Later, when Uncle Bill and his wife, Monnie, had their fiftieth wedding anniversary, we went back to Madrid, which is a ghost town now and open as a tourist attraction. We were eating in a restaurant there, and I happened to mention to the waitress, who was the daughter of the owner, that we had pictures that my mother had taken when they lived there. She asked me to send them to her, so when I got home, I had copies made of them and sent the copies to her.

Mother was in school from fifth to seventh grade there and did well. She was very good at math, loved history, and did exceptionally well in reading. She also had to take over the management of the house at that time. Grandmother started working at the boarding house, not because they needed the money (Granddad always made good money) but because she wanted to get out of the house. Mother made the younger girls help her. I remember, as a child, her talking about making her younger sisters help with the ironing. Most of it fell on Mother, but Aunt Mary would iron her own clothes and make them look nice. Aunt Emily, who was very young at that time, wouldn't iron her clothes, but since she was ten years younger than Mother, that isn't surprising. I think she told me that because I didn't like to iron (still don't), and she had to practically force me to do it.

It was during that time Mother learned to sew. She told me about making a dress for herself. She got the material from the company store, came home, laid one of her dresses out on the bed, on the material and cut it out. This is how she had seen her mother cut out a dress. When it was made, it was too small for her. She was always a chubby child, and Aunt Mary was very slender. To her dismay, the dress just fit Mary, so she wore it.

It was there also where she learned to cook. Grandmother was what Mother called a good, plain cook. Grandad didn't like fried food, so they usually boiled or baked the food.

Grandmother was very good at making pastry and bread and taught Mother that when she was very young.

I also need to address their religious training, which, from what I gathered, was practically nonexistent. Granddad had been raised in a very religious home. His grandfather was a Methodist minister, and his father was an elder in the church. He was sent to the Methodist college at Fort Worth, Texas when he was old enough, but the family didn't have enough money the next year to send both him and his sister, Sylvia, so Granddad sent her with the understanding that after that year, she would teach and send him to school for at least one year. At the end of the year, she got married, stating to him that her year at school was his wedding present to her. He never forgave her. While there, he had a teacher who was an atheist, who managed to convince him that there is no God.

I don't know much about Grandmother's religious training. I do know they lived in the country, and it may have been difficult for them to go to church. She told me that she was "practically a heathen" until she became involved with Sister Aimee Semple McPherson, which was long after she and Granddad had separated. When they had lived in Clovis, the children were sent to Sunday School. Both Mother and Aunt Mary told me about their first Sunday there. Grandmother got them ready and sent them to the nearest church, which was a Baptist church, I think. As they approached, they were met by a lady who told them that this wasn't the church for them, to go on down the street to the other church, which they did.

Most of the people in Madrid were "foreigners" of Italian or southeastern European descent. They were mostly Catholic because that was the only church there, but some of the ladies had organized a Union Sunday School, which taught only the Bible. Mother and the other children attended that, and it wasn't until much later that Mother began to have any real interest in religious things. The Pentecostal "hoop-la," as she termed it, turned her off, but Mary and Bill both followed Grandmother into it and were faithful all their lives. I'm not sure when she joined the Episcopalian church, but she said she liked their reverence and quietness, so that's what she practiced until she joined the Adventist church in Stanley many years later.

I'm not sure just why they left Madrid. It probably was because of my grandfather's hot temper. He wasn't one to take anything off anyone. He quit more good jobs over that than anything else. He didn't seem to have any trouble finding another job, but it did mean that they moved frequently. They never really packed up, never took any furniture with them, only their personal possessions, which meant that they had a somewhat unstable childhood. Mother said that they stayed at Madrid longer than any other place during her childhood, and she was the happiest there. She didn't like having to make new friends and became somewhat reserved, a characteristic she carried throughout the rest of her life. It was when they left Madrid that the actual separation between Grandmother and Granddad occurred. They never lived together again from that time on. The children were with either one or the other. Most of the time, the girls, except Mother, were with Grandmother and the boys with their father, I think. I think it was at that time that Mother became such a private person. She was able to avoid questions without giving offence, something that I have never been able to do.

THE KINGMAN YEARS

They moved to Kingman, Arizona, sometime that summer. Mother talked about going to school in Kingman in the eighth grade. The eighth grade class was held in the basement of the high school. I do know that her mother and sisters were there with her that year, but I don't know where Granddad and the boys were.

Before school started the following fall, Granddad took a job in a mine in the southern part of Arizona. Meanwhile, Grandmother moved to Ft. Mojave, which was further north, to run the boarding house there. Since that county had only one high school, and it was located in Kingman, about fifty miles away to the east, Mother, who was a freshman at this point, had to stay nearby, as did all the other kids who lived out of town. Most of the other children from out of town lived with different families there in Kingman, but Mother's family didn't have any close friends or family with whom she could stay, so Granddad asked some of the men to recommend a good place to board. Whoever he was talking to recommended The Graystone Inn, so Granddad secured a room for Mother there, which was a place full of men. Fortunately, Mother wasn't sexually mature. She said she still liked to play with dolls at that point, so being exposed to all the men in the inn didn't lead to any harm. Later in life she shuddered to think what could have happened.

For the first two to three months, she said she lived like a "lady of leisure," but then Granddad lost his job. He had been living in a boarding house close to where he was working in southern Arizona, and the woman who ran it fried almost everything. He didn't like fried food, so he was living on candy and sweets from the store. When they did a physical on him, among other things, they tested his urine for sugar, which was loaded with it. They told him he had "diabetes in the worst way," and he wasn't expected to live very long. He wired Mother to meet him at the depot, so she did. She said he was really a sad sight. He hadn't eaten anything since he had heard about his diabetes and was, among other things, very hungry. They went to a store nearby, and he got a can of spinach, opened it with his knife and sat down to eat it. "I don't think this will hurt me," he told her, as he ate it.

I think he went to stay with his brother, Uncle Tommy, who was working in another mine there in Arizona, but it wasn't long until he was working again. He said that he saw an advertisement in a magazine about that time for some kind of cactus juice that was guaranteed to cure diabetes. He wanted to get it, but he didn't have the money. If he had gotten it, he would have sworn that it did cure him. The truth was that he didn't have diabetes. His blood sugar was high simply because he was eating too much candy.

Since Granddad could no longer pay her board bill, Mother went to the owner of the Graystone Inn, a Mrs. English, and asked if she could work for her room and board. She did get the job, so from that time on, she was self-supporting. She helped serve the breakfast and supper meals (the men took lunches with them), cleaned the dining room after the meals, and they changed all the beds and gave each room a good cleaning on Saturdays. In the evenings she did babysitting to give her the additional money she needed. She did most of her studying at school during her library time.

Mother said that she never had to work in the kitchen because Mrs. English always had a "bum" to do the dishes. She commented several times on how filthy the kitchen was, although the rest of the house was nice and clean, but Mrs. English turned out good food. Apparently, she also had a very filthy mouth and a hot temper, but since Mother was used to hearing so much fighting at home, she had learned to ignore that. She never talked much about the other students at the school, only that there were about 100 in the whole high school. She did say that the Catholic priest, who lived next door, either ran an extension or loaned them his radio, so they could listen to it. That may have been where she developed her love for classical music.

That first year, shortly after school started, she and another girl were walking down the hall when one of the teachers grabbed them. "I need two more students in my art class," she told them. "If I don't get them, they are going to close it for this year." Mother said she and the other girl looked at each other and agreed to add this to their other classes. That meant she was taking five solids that year. She had no problems carrying them, so the next year, she signed up for five again. This was her sophomore year. Remember, she was eight when she started school, which may have been part of the reason she did so well.

It was sometime during the following summer that Grandmother decided to move to Albuquerque. She insisted that Mother go with her, although Mother could never figure out why. She had been completely self-supporting for the past two years and certainly could have continued doing it, but Grandmother insisted, and being an obedient child, Mother obeyed.

THE ALBUQUERQUE AND LAS VEGAS YEARS

Shortly after they arrived in Albuquerque, Grandmother started working at the boarding house at Golden, a small mining town northeast of Albuquerque. Mother started school at Albuquerque High, which was a much larger school than the one in Kingman. Since Grandmother wasn't there, she found Mother a room with a lady who took boarders. Mother never said anything about working that year, so I don't think she did. I do know that she hated the school. She knew no one there and, apparently, didn't try to make any friends. I can't imagine my mother ever sulking, but if she ever did, it was at that time. Again, she signed up for five classes. She could tell you what they were for each year, but I don't remember. I do know that she took English and a math class each year; she really liked math.

At midterm, they had to sign up again, and she did, taking the same things she had taken the previous semester. As she said, she had to have a teacher sign the schedule, and looking around, she didn't see any of her teachers, so she went to another teacher, a man who looked it over. He had her transcript, and after looking it over, he turned to her and said, "Do you realize that after this year, you are going to lack only one credit of being able to graduate?"

Mother, who was never really quick with a response, said a very hesitant "No."

He then asked her, "Do you want to come back all next year for only one subject?"

Again, she said, "No, I guess not."

He said, "Okay, let's see what you lack." After checking, he determined that the only required subject she didn't have was American History. There was a class of first semester American History starting a class of kids who had failed the first semester. So, he put her in that. It interfered with one of the other classes she was taking, so he had to change that, which caused him to have to change another class, and it ended up with him changing her whole schedule. The other teachers weren't too happy about that, but he insisted. She said it was interesting because that American History class was made up of kids who really didn't care if they passed or not. The teacher was an elderly woman who couldn't begin to handle them. There were many days when she stood there with tears in her eyes and a helpless look on her face. Of course, since Mother was a good student, she really stood out. Mother said several of the same boys were in her French class and when they tried their nonsense on that teacher, they were quickly brought back in line. Mother said it only took a stern look from that teacher.

The only other thing I can remember Mother talking about that year was when she was given some money and went down and bought a new purse, which took all her money, so there she was, with a new purse and nothing to put in it.

She finished that school year, then had to take the other semester of American History that summer, and another class to make up the credit she lacked. She said she didn't realize that every day of summer school was the same as three days during the regular session. She signed up for American History to finish it, an English class of some kind, and second year Algebra. She said she nearly worked herself to death that summer. She had to write a long paper for her English class, and anytime a person has to work on 150 algebra problems, no matter how good they are at math, it takes time. But she finished with good grades. She finished high school, but she didn't have a graduation ceremony.

Now, it was time for her to go to college. Granddad wanted her to become a doctor. In fact, he had insisted that she take Latin in high school for that very reason. One of his ancestors was related to Dr. Elizabeth Blackwell, the first female doctor in the United States, and he wanted

Mother to follow in her footsteps. Mother could have easily done it, but she wasn't really interested in studying medicine. Finally, her mother said that if she wanted to go to Las Vegas, New Mexico, to the normal training school there, she would pay for it, so Mother and Uncle John headed north to Las Vegas. Remember, this was in the 1920s, and most teachers were women, so the school was made up of mostly girls. At first, she lived in the college dorm, but within a month or two, they rented an apartment and lived there through the rest of the school year. Being one of a very few boys in the school, Uncle John had his pick of the girls and apparently had a fairly active social life that year.

She talked about how she and Uncle John joined a choir, and they presented Handel's "Messiah." She really enjoyed that as well as some of the other songs they sang. As far as I know, that was the only time she sang much, other than being in the Glee Club in Kingman. She had a pleasant singing voice but nothing outstanding. Her mother had learned to play the piano when she was young, but the Wells weren't a very musical family, from what I gather.

At the end of the year, her landlady spoke to the superintendent of schools, who was a friend, and he gave Mother a school to teach. She had taken no classes on teaching and should never have accepted the school, but she was very pleased to know that she could teach, so she accepted it. Other than taking classes in the summer, that was the only college training she had.

> *At the end of the year, her landlady spoke to the superintendent of schools, who was a friend, and he gave Mother a school to teach. She had taken no classes on teaching and should never have accepted the school, but she was very pleased to know that she could teach, so she accepted it.*

THE TEACHING YEARS

Mother said she was really flattered when the superintendent offered her a school. She wondered later if her main attraction to him was the fact that she couldn't speak Spanish. He sent her to the little town of Nambe, a town that is close to Espanola. Apparently, the previous teachers all taught the children in Spanish, and the superintendent, being aware of it, decided to send a teacher who would teach the children in English, which she did. I'm not sure they learned much more that year, but they did learn correct English. She realized shortly after arriving there that she needed some training in how to teach. She said that she had to try to remember how her teachers had taught her, especially in the first two grades and tried to do that. It was a nice experience for her, and she enjoyed it.

She took some more classes that next summer, then she was given the school at Carnahan, a town that was built for a mine also in northern New Mexico. Grandmother was running the boarding house there, so she stayed with her, and Uncle Billy and Aunt Emily were in the school. The mine closed during the year, and as the people left, they took their children with them, of course. She started out with about thirty students, and at the end of the school year, there were about seven left, the children of ranchers who lived nearby. That was the last year that school existed.

Mother started out fairly well, but as the year progressed, things got worse. One big problem, for her, was the fact that she was teaching Billy and Emily. Of course, they called her Rebecca, so the other children did, too. From that time on, she never allowed anyone to call her by her first name. Even when she was old, everyone called her either Mrs. or Sister Ivie.

I don't think Billy and Emily gave her much trouble, but there were others that did, and she grew to actually hate the school. She said that she would pray every night that the schoolhouse would burn down. Of course, it didn't, and she finished teaching that year. Since it was only her second year of teaching, she didn't have the experience to handle the problems that arose. She said that if she had been more experienced, she would never have let things get so out of hand. Part of the problem was the mixture of children, about evenly divided between Spanish-speaking and English-speaking students. They were at war, and each accused her of siding with the other ones, and she didn't have the experience to stop it. When that school year ended, she vowed she would NEVER teach again, so she didn't go to summer school and didn't apply for another school. She spent that summer with her father and, as she put it, lived a life of ease. However, over the summer months, her feelings had moderated, and when she was offered another school, she accepted it.

It was at that time that Granddad insisted that she learn to drive and made her get a car.

Uncle Billy was with them, so the two of them went into Albuquerque, and she bought a Willis. She said she thought Uncle Billy expected to do most of the driving. In fact, he thought the car would be mostly for him, so he picked out a little roadster, a two-seater, which was not what she needed. Granddad "taught" her to drive. This must have been interesting, since he barely knew how to drive himself, and he didn't drive if he could help it. But she managed to grasp the fundamentals, although she was never a very good driver and certainly didn't enjoy driving.

When she left to go to Santa Fe to learn information about her new school, she was decidedly nervous. She said she drove about 10-15 mph, so it took her most of the day to drive about forty miles. I'm not sure where she taught next. She could tell, but I don't remember. I do know that she taught at Stanley one year. She told me that while she was there Mrs. Fisher talked to her about the clean meats, showing her in Leviticus 11 where they were listed and her going home and throwing out her ham and bacon, but it didn't last. Those were pleasant years; she had some good memories and some that weren't so good.

To show how she had become a strong disciplinarian, she talked about the state deciding that the children needed a tablespoon of cod liver oil every morning. They sent her a big bottle, and she was instructed to give it to them. She said she would go down the line, have each child hold up his/her mouth, and she would pour in the cod liver oil from her tablespoon, then go on to the next child.

She also talked about some of the older boys deciding to make trouble in one of the schools, I don't remember which one. She found out ahead of time and stopped by one of the neighbors' houses to get a belt. She always considered it a defeat when she had to spank a child, but she would if necessary and thought it might be necessary that day. Apparently, the neighbor told the father of the boy who was the ringleader of the problem. Just before noon the father came to the school. He asked Mother how things were going, and she answered that they were doing fine, so he turned to look at the students and said, "I'm really glad to hear that. If you have any problems, you just let me know, and you will have my full support."

Mother said the boy, when his father came into the room, looked really pleased and looked at the other boys as if to say, "See, I told you so," but when his father looked at him and declared he was going to support Mother, he just wilted. There was no trouble that day, or any other, either. However, not all the parents were so supportive. Later, at another school, she had to discipline a little girl. She usually stayed late to grade the papers, so she was still there when the mother arrived.

She said the schoolhouse was at the top of a little hill, so the mother, who was somewhat overweight, was really puffing when she arrived. She was out of breath, but that didn't stop her. She lit into Mother immediately. She didn't like what had happened; she didn't want anyone treating her precious daughter in that manner and would appreciate it if Mother would stop treating her darling like that. When Mother tried to explain what had happened, her only answer was, "That's not what my daughter told me, and I believe her." Mother said she never said another word. If that was the woman's attitude, there was no sense in pursuing it further.

Mother talked about her boarding one year with a family named Brown. She had a lot of respect for Mrs. Brown. Mr. Brown was a widower with several children, two girls and a boy or two. It was the girls that were the problem. Apparently, before he remarried, someone told the children that they were getting a stepmother, and she would be very mean to them. At the time Mother was there, the girls were in their early teens, I think.

Mother said it looked like, to her, that they sat around trying to think of ways to torment Mrs. Brown.

Mrs. Brown was very good to them and tried in every way to please them. She had been a businesswoman before her marriage and had some really nice clothes. She made them over for the girls, so they would have nice clothes to wear to school. Another example she gave was when Mrs. Brown asked one of the girls, who was born in the wintertime, what kind of cake she wanted for her birthday. The girl asked for a strawberry shortcake. There were no frozen strawberries back then, and Mrs. Brown almost made herself sick, worrying about getting some strawberries. She finally found some that were canned, so she was able to give the girl her strawberry shortcake for her birthday. Mother said the girl looked anything but pleased when she brought it to the table. It was then that Mother decided she would never marry a man who had children. Fortunately, when they were older, the girls began to realize how good Mrs. Brown had been to them, and after they left home, they were very good to Mrs. Brown.

She talked about a friend she had—a girl named Sarah. Since Mother had a car, she was somewhat popular with the young people. Apparently, Sarah wasn't the serious person that Mother was. She told me about taking Sarah into Santa Fe and stopping at a store before they got to their destination to get a pair of hose for Sarah. It was during those years that Mother learned to be so very careful with her money. Most of the teachers had to borrow money to live through the summer because they were only paid nine months of the year, but Mother always saved enough to keep her going during the summer months.

It was during that time that Mother took on the responsibility of helping Billy and Emily. Her brother, John, had gone to Texas Tech and got a degree in engineering. Mary had gone to a secretarial school and became a secretary. I don't know who told Granddad this. Aunt Mary was never very fast, but her shorthand was, as he stated, "Copper plate." She would have done well as a teacher in a secretarial school.

She arranged for Uncle Billy to go to a boarding school at El Rito, a small town in northern New Mexico. Since she didn't have enough money for his personal needs after paying his entrance fees, getting him settled, getting him some decent clothes, etc., she said she got several magazines and cut out the coupons for such things as toothpaste, deodorant, and bath soap. At that time, the companies would put a coupon as advertising in the magazines, and all a person had to do was send in the coupon, and the company would send a sample by mail. So, Uncle Billy got his first month's supply via mail. After mother got her first paycheck, he had a regular supply.

It was also during these years that she finally became interested in the opposite sex and started dating. As I said, since she had a car, she was somewhat popular. In looking through her photograph album once, I saw a picture of her with a young man and asked her who he was. She said his name was Bruce and that they had dated for about three years. I asked her why they hadn't gotten married, and she said that during the depression a lot of people didn't marry because they didn't have any money.

She met my father, named Oscar Elgin Ivie, through one of her students. Daddy had just been discharged from the army in Texas, where he had served as a cook. Upon his discharge, he had gone to New Mexico to visit his two uncles and their families. Herbert, his cousin, was a great admirer of Mother, his teacher, and when Daddy arrived, he was determined to bring the two of them together. Daddy told me that just a day or two after he arrived, Herbert asked Daddy to go for a ride with him on horseback, then he took off like an arrow for the schoolhouse, where Mother was doing some work. I'm not sure how long they dated, but I do know they were married on her birthday in Santa Fe by a minister in the minister's home. There were no other witnesses, and their marriage wasn't published because Mother wanted to teach the coming year.

Mother said that she fully expected Daddy to join her in attending church and to eventually be baptized, but that never happened. I know that she was quite eager to share with him her new belief even though he obviously wasn't really interested. She did go with him to church on Sunday, since she wanted him to join her in attending Sabbath School, which he never did. He was raised in the Primitive Baptist Church (also called "the Hard-shell Baptist") and could never accept anything else.

For those of you who are unfamiliar with the Primitive Baptist Church, they are a small group that is dying out. They do not believe in evangelizing; there is no musical instrument in their churches; they don't believe in Sunday School or paid pastors. Most of Daddy's family were raised in that church, and they taught him well.

She told me about the event that finally convinced her that he had no real interest in religion. They were on their way to church one Sunday, and for some reason stopped to talk with someone who told Daddy that they were going to play baseball. Daddy immediately lost all interest in going to church, so they went to the baseball game instead. They spent that Sunday and most other Sundays with Daddy playing baseball instead of going to church. Daddy was very good at playing baseball. He was, in fact, invited to join one of the minor leagues and didn't understand that that was the pathway to the major leagues, so he refused to try out for them. I asked Daddy one time what he thought about Mother's devotion to, as he put it, her church. He said that he always wanted a wife who had a strong belief in God and would raise his children that way. What he hadn't counted on was the total commitment Mother gave to God.

> *I asked Daddy one time what he thought about Mother's devotion to, as he put it, her church. He said that he always wanted a wife who had a strong belief in God and would raise his children that way. What he hadn't counted on was the total commitment Mother gave to God.*

During the school year, Daddy had gotten the job of driving the school bus to pick up the children who lived out of town. This was during the Great Depression, so he was willing to do any kind of work that was honorable to earn a living. He told me about finding a ditch one morning that had been dug across one of the roads he needed to travel to get to one of the farms. Since the shovel was there, he got out, filled in the ditch two places, drove over it, and went on. He said it took him about ten to fifteen minutes to do it. Later that day, he heard one of the men in town talking about that "sorry man who had done two men out of a day's work by filling in that ditch." He had nothing but contempt for the men who worked on the Public Works Administration. He also talked about a conversation he had with one of the neighbors later. He asked how he was doing. The neighbor said he was panning for gold on a stream that ran fairly close to his house. Daddy asked him how much he was finding. His answer was, "I'm getting about a dime a day, but it beats going on relief."

THE EARLY MARRIED YEARS

I suppose it was after Mother and Daddy were engaged that Daddy wrote to his sister, Aunt Ruby, and told her of their pending nuptials. Aunt Ruby was happy for him. He was twenty-eight, and she thought it was time he settled down. She asked for a picture of Mother. I don't know where he found it, but he sent a picture of a black woman. (Daddy was a great tease.) Aunt Ruby wrote back that since that was his choice, she would welcome her into the family. The whole family was very racist and were very much against "mixed marriages."

Sometime after they were married, probably during one of the vacations during that school year, they went to Texas so Daddy could show off his new bride. It was after dark when they arrived at Mineral Wells, Texas. Daddy knocked at the door, then stepped back behind mother where the light from the open door wouldn't shine on him. When Aunt Ruby opened the door, she saw only Mother and had no idea who she was. Mother waited for Daddy to introduce her, but he wasn't in sight, so she wasn't sure what to do. Then Daddy started laughing at the expression on their faces.

When the school year ended, Mother joined Daddy in the little place he had rented for that year. She didn't talk much about it, except to say that the house was very small and full of bedbugs. She put the legs of the bed in little cans of kerosine and that helped somewhat, but the bedbugs would drop from the ceiling, so every day she had to take the mattress outside and leave it in the sunlight. She managed to hold them in check that way. It was while they were living there that John Kenneth, my brother, was born. I think it was the next year that Daddy found the place they lived at until he went into the Marines in 1942. It had been abandoned.

Daddy paid the taxes on it at least one year, then discovered that he could get the title if he paid all the back taxes, but there was a problem because he had paid taxes on it without trying to get the title. He wanted to put it in his sister Ruby's name, but she lived in Texas, so Mother suggested putting it in her father's name, which he did. It was the beginning of the animosity between them. Granddad had always wanted a place of his own. In fact, at least two different times, he had made the down payment on a place, then given Grandmother the money to make the payments on it, which she didn't do. She said she would never live on a farm again and was determined to avoid it. The agreement was that after a certain period, probably about two to three years, Granddad would put the place back in Daddy's name, but he never did and always called it his. However, it did come to us children when he realized he was too old to live there by himself.

There had previously been a house on the property, but just the walls and floor were all that remained, so Daddy got canvas and made a roof out of that. It was very small, and Mother said he used up more than half of it by storing his hay there. It was also very hard to heat. When Granddad came to visit them, he took some time off from work and built them an adobe house. He told me about mixing the mud on a red ant bed, pouring water on it and mixing it with his bare feet. The ants stung him until his legs were really swollen. I don't think he realized that red ants have the same poison that rattlesnakes have or he might not have chosen that spot to mix the mud. The house was small but warm, and Daddy could use the "tent house" as a barn for his hay.

The place had a well with good water. When the previous owners had dug the well, they went down about 30 feet and found nothing, but there was a spot on the side at about 20 feet that was really wet, so they tunneled there and hit a stream. It quickly filled the hole and was a good well for many years. Water is very precious in that area, and good wells are a rarity.

Mother told of another family who dug almost 600 feet and didn't find water.

The house had only "two rooms and a path," so Daddy had to build a privy, and until he could get that done, he dug the hole and built the frame to sit on, but he leaned some boards against it to give a little bit of privacy.

The next day, he was sitting there when he heard a car coming into the yard. In trying to see who was there, he managed to knock the boards down, and there he was, very exposed. It was his uncle and cousin, and they teased him about that many times.

Mother always said those were good years for them. It wasn't a very prosperous farm, but it met their needs, and, as Mother said, if they needed something, they could always sell a calf or something. They never had to really do without. Also, since the state paid the teachers out of the taxes, and most people didn't have the money for the taxes, they sent the teachers what Mother called "vouchers." When the state got the money, they would redeem them for full price. However, many of the teachers went to the stores that would pay them seventy-five cents on the dollar and sold them. Mother never did, so she eventually got her full salary. That's why when Aunt Emily went back to SWJC, she owed seventy-five cents. Since Mother had agreed to help Aunt Emily with her school bill, she had paid the bill but somehow neglected to pay the last seventy-five cents.

> Mother always said those were good years for them. It wasn't a very prosperous farm, but it met their needs, and, as Mother said, if they needed something, they could always sell a calf or something. They never had to really do without.

It was shortly after the house was finished that, as Mother was working in the house, she heard a truck stop then start up again. The house was located in a small draw, so the road climbed up going either way. There was no truck in sight, but there was a man walking up to the house. Her first thought was that it was Granddad, that someone had dropped him off and traveled on up the road. She rushed outside, ran down to him and was about to throw her arms around his neck, when she realized it was one of the neighbor men who had come to get a barrel of water. She never told me what she said or did, but I know she must have been embarrassed.

My brother, named John Kenneth, for her father, was born the previous September. His birthday is September 12, 1935. Daddy said the doctor gave Mother something to hurry the process, so he wouldn't be born on the 13th. He was born in Albuquerque at the Women's and Children's Hospital. Since he was the first grandchild, Granddad paid for him. Mother tried to breastfeed him, but she was following the book she had gotten from somewhere on how to raise children. It said to keep them on a strict four-hour schedule. He would cry until she fed him, but she didn't produce enough milk to keep him from being hungry again He would fall asleep but was hungry well before the four hours were over. He almost starved. Grandmother came, saw what was happening, and insisted she put him on a bottle. That ended the problem. Mother said later that if she had put him to the breast more often, she might have brought in more milk.

It was about that time that Daddy decided that the Willis car was too small, so he traded it off to one of his relatives for a pickup. He really got a raw deal. The car was a good car, and the pickup was not worth much. It gave him nothing but trouble. He finally had to just junk it. I'm not sure if they ever got another vehicle or not. I do know that when he joined the Marine Corp, they had no car or truck.

Mother, being raised in towns with electricity, was used to more modern things. With some of her money, she bought a washing machine that ran on a little gasoline motor. Being the generous person she was, she invited the other farm women to come use it, rather than the rub board they were used to. They did, one by one, then went home and insisted that their husbands get them a washing machine also. Daddy said all of the men around there were mad at him because they had to spend some of their few dollars on a washing machine for their wives. It was also about that time that Mother got her first sewing machine. It was a Singer treadle machine. It had been used as a demonstrator and was sold very much below asking price. She taught me to sew on it, and until Granddad moved in with us in 1950, we used the treadle. At that time, he put a motor on it. She earned a lot of money with that machine over the years.

Sometime after my brother, John, was born, Daddy's father came for a visit. He had

> Mother, being raised in towns with electricity, was used to more modern things. With some of her money, she bought a washing machine that ran on a little gasoline motor. Being the generous person she was, she invited the other farm women to come use it, rather than the rub board they were used to. They did, one by one, then went home and insisted that their husbands get them a washing machine also. Daddy said all of the men around there were mad at him because they had to spend some of their few dollars on a washing machine for their wives.

lived most of his life in Texas and Oklahoma, so he wasn't used to the dryer climate. As he put it, "This can't be very good land here. You can't even grow decent cactus." Mother wasn't used to being around a dour Scotsman, who would sit for hours and not say a word. Granddad would talk to himself if no one was around. Granddad Ivie was very taken with John and would sit for hours holding him. He was the youngest of his grandchildren and was a very cute baby. He was there for about a month, I was told, then went back to live with one of his sons in Texas, where he died a short time later, before I was born.

I was born in February of 1938. They had gone into Albuquerque earlier because the weather can be quite severe there. They stayed with Grandmother, who was renting an apartment, two rooms, from an old couple. I don't know what their real name was, but we called them Mr. and Mrs. Nick. Mother told Daddy he had to stay with her until the baby was born since she knew that her mother would be useless in that situation, and as it turned out, she was right. When Mother knew I was on the way, Daddy called the doctor, who came and examined her. He said things were going well, that he would go on to the hospital, then stop back on his way to the office. He did and still was satisfied with Mother's progress. He said he would stop on his way home for lunch if they hadn't called him before then, so he left.

Shortly before noon, Mother knew that I was arriving, so Daddy called the doctor's office, but he had already left. Before he arrived, I did. As usual, Grandmother went into hysterics. Daddy said it was bedlam; Grandmother standing there, wringing her hands, Mother trying to get up to calm her, and Daddy trying to push Mother back down. Finally, Mrs. Nick took Grandmother by the hand and led her out, saying, "Come along, deary. Let's go get a cup of tea." They left, and Daddy delivered me. Shortly after that, the doctor arrived, and after finding that I was bleeding from a cut in the cord, redressed it and then sat down to write out the birth certificate.

"And what are we going to name her?" he asked Daddy, who was still rather upset by the whole incident.

The date was February 22, George Washington's birthday, and Daddy was sitting there, with his head in his hands, saying, "George, ah, George, ah," trying to remember the name of Martha, who was George's wife. When he turned to the doctor to give him the name Martha, the doctor had already written down Georgia. That's how I got my name. In case you are wondering why they hadn't picked out a girl's name before, Mother had said she was going to have six boys. I was a surprise and a big disappointment to her. Oddly enough, she later had two more girls. John was the only son they had.

From the very first, she started us studying the Bible. She subscribed to *The Little Friend* for us, and we studied the lesson every night before we went to bed. By the time we could talk, she had us memorizing the memory verses. We always kept the Sabbath. She tried to make it a very special day, and we always looked forward to the Sabbath. Many years later, Grandmother told of an incident that happened when I was about three. We had gone into Albuquerque for a visit and were there over the Sabbath. Grandmother asked me if I wanted to go with her to get some ice cream. Being a very young child, I, of course, wanted it, so I went to ask Mother if I could go. I didn't return for some time, and when I did, Grandmother asked me why I hadn't come back. She said I looked up at her and said, very solemnly, "But Grandmother, it's the Sabbath." It made such an impression on her that years later, when I had children of my own, she remembered it.

Those were busy years for Mother. It was her responsibility to take care of the livestock, milk the cows, and turn them out to pasture. They had two horses that Daddy used for plowing: Babe and Mable. Mable was a very steady horse, but Babe had gotten into some Loco weed and tended to be erratic. It was years later that I learned that Loco weed was another name for marijuana. When we were old enough, and it was warm weather, she would put me and John on the backs of the cows and let us ride, either to or from the pasture. This worked well until Daddy brought in two cows, I think, that were not used to children. Mother, without thinking, tried to put one of us on her back and was kicked out of the barn for her efforts. From what Granddad told me later, that caused her first miscarriage.

Mother said I was a real problem from the time I was born. I was a colicky baby, was always spitting up, and Mother said I always smelled like sour milk. When I got out of that stage, I was always into everything. She said one of my favorite things to do when she had to leave us in the house during cold weather was to get a jar of Vaseline or cold cream and "polish the furniture." One of my few memories from that time is standing at the door and yelling with John, just to hear how our voices sounded together. I think I was about three when I decided to follow Mother one evening when she went to get the cows. She had gone up the hill, and I couldn't see her, so I just went where I thought she might have gone. It wasn't too long until I became tired, so I sat down and then went to sleep. When she got back to the house, I was missing. It ended up with two of the neighbor families helping her look for me. I was finally found when I awoke and, it being dark, became frightened and decided to return home. I was adventuresome and wasn't afraid of much (I'm still not), and I could think of more things to get into than any other child she had been around. She wouldn't stand for any disobedience, but I still managed to get into plenty of trouble.

On the other hand, John was a very good child. He was obedient and helpful from an early age. Fortunately, she had him first. If she had had me first, she probably would never have wanted any more children. She said that she was used to handling children after they were old enough to go to school, but she felt completely lost with tiny children. Her favorite age was around ten years old, when kids were in the third or fourth grades.

It was the year that I was born that Daddy started working at the Veterans' Hospital in Albuquerque as an orderly. Because of the drought, they were unable to make much money raising the pinto beans, which is what everyone raised there, so Daddy accepted that job. He worked there, other than the war years, until he retired in 1965. He must have stayed in town and come home on his days off, since they continued to keep the place. He worked on the tuberculosis ward and was always afraid of carrying it home to us. He was a hard worker and did well at it and was a valued employee until his health forced him to retire.

We left the farm when I was four, so my actual memories of it are very few. Most of what I have related are things that were told to me once I was older.

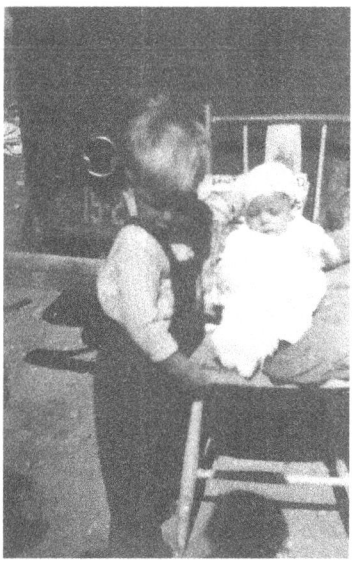

John and Georgia in 1938.

THE WAR YEARS

When the Japanese bombed Pearl Harbor, they didn't realize that they had unleashed so much animosity against them. Almost every man in the United States tried to enlist, including my grandfather who was sixty-five at that time. Daddy, Mother said, "thought they couldn't win the war without him," so he was one of the first to enlist. Since he had previously been in the army, he didn't have to go through basic training. He joined the Marine Corp under a special class of older men who were former military men or police officers. Their job was to do guard duty in the United States to allow the younger men to go overseas. He was first stationed in San Diego, but because of the fear of being attacked along the west coast, they were advised to not bring their families out, so Mother and we children stayed in New Mexico.

However, Mother didn't want to stay on the farm. She was left there with two small children, no vehicle, and pregnant. She wrote to Granddad and asked him about moving to Magdalena with him. Granddad had moved to Magdalena, New Mexico, to work in the mine there when they had refused to let him enlist. The quality of metal (I think it was zinc) in that mine was so poor that it only paid to operate it during a war, so it wasn't a main industry of the town. As usual, he was overjoyed to have her with him, so we moved there. The house that he had found was an old, abandoned shack on the side of the hill, overlooking the town, which was in the valley below. In fact, the ground sloped down underneath the house, so it was supported by piles to make the floor of the house level. This made for a good place for children to play out of the sun. It consisted of three rooms and "a path." We had no electricity, so we just used coal oil lamps. We got our water from a fifty-five-gallon barrel. I remember one morning finding a drowned rat in the barrel and watching as Granddad dumped the barrel. Mother cooked on a coal stove, and we slept in the living room. Granddad and Aunt Emily also shared the house with us. It was there that mother, while chopping wood one day badly cut her big toe. Either the log slipped or her foot did because when she brought the ax down, it almost cut her toe in half, down the middle. She said later that she ran in the house, took off her shoe, wrapped a dishcloth around her foot, and just fell into bed. One of her regrets was that she had ruined a good pair of shoes.

The mine was some distance from the railroad, so the ore was carried overhead in what was called "gondolas" or big buckets. The house wasn't far from these, so we children were cautioned to always look to see if a gondola was coming before we crossed under the line. One day, as we were nearing the line, we saw one of the gondolas fall. Being young and very excited, we went running to see Aunt Emily, who worked in the office. After listening to us, she told us to go and that we were good for obeying her and looking. As we left the office, as I heard many years later, the foreman came to her and asked, "What were those two kids so excited about?" When Aunt Emily told him, he asked why he hadn't been informed of that. Her answer was all she knew was what we had told her, so he went to do some investigating. As we said, the bucket had fallen. The men were trying to keep it from his knowledge since it was their fault. I expect they were pretty peeved with us for telling on them.

Within a month or two of us moving to Magdalena, mother had another miscarriage. While I was only four at the time, I do remember her having to stay in bed. As I said, we slept in the front room. I was in there playing one morning when Mother called me to the bed and told me to stay there. A large rattlesnake was across the room and there was no one there except Mother and me. She couldn't get up, and it was going to be some time before either Aunt Emily or Granddad came. I can remember her taking some notepaper she had there, making little balls of it, and throwing them at the snake. However, that's where my memory of the incident ends. I suppose someone came and dispatched the snake. Another time, John was outside playing on a pile of lumber. Granddad came and John told him that when he jumped on a certain board there was a funny noise. Granddad listened, moved the board, and killed the rattlesnake that was under it. Obviously, there was a good supply of rattlesnakes in that area.

It was either shortly before we moved there, or after we moved there, that we went to camp meeting. Until then, Mother hadn't had the money to attend, but now she was getting money each month from Daddy's service. Camp meeting was held in Clovis, New Mexico, at the high school auditorium that year. We rented a room from one of the town people and walked each day to the meetings. Why I was with Mother in the auditorium, I don't know. Surely, they had children's classes, but I was with her. Because I wasn't used to sitting in church, I, who was a restless child at best, became a problem, so she sent me outside to play. The gymnasium was on the second floor, with wide steps leading up to it. I, as children will do, climbed up on the railing, which was concrete, and was walking on it when I fell. Fortunately, it wasn't cemented below, or it probably would have killed me. It did knock me out, and I don't know how long it was before I recovered enough to crawl around to the steps, where I passed out again. Someone saw me lying there and told Mother that I had rolled down the steps. I'm sure most of my upper face was bruised. I obviously had a severe concussion and several of the people there tried to get her to take me to see a doctor, but she said she was afraid she didn't have enough money to pay for that, so she didn't. Of course, I had a terrific headache and was crying.

Mother told me that if I would stop crying, she would buy me a book, and I did. We went into the bookstore, and she got me one of the series of Uncle Arthur's Bedtime Stories. It had a red cover, and I enjoyed listening to the stories in it for many years. (Incidentally, I still have the deep crack in my head. It goes from the middle of my skull, down almost to the orbit of my eye, where my skull was fractured.)

As I said, the building at Magdalena was old, and among other things, the roof leaked. Granddad managed to find some five-gallon cans. He cut the top and bottom out of them and flattened them out to put on the roof. He placed a one by twelve board against the roof as a ladder and sent John up to help him get them up on the roof, and, I, being the brat I was, went up to "help" him. He didn't want my help, and we got into a small tussling contest, which ended up by putting the corner of one of the cans into my leg. I came down with my leg bleeding freely and me letting the whole world know that I was hurt. Mother wrapped a dishcloth around my leg, and Aunt Emily, who was there, drove us to the doctor's office. Magdalena had only two traffic lights, and neither one had a yellow light. It went from green to red—remember this was in 1942. As she approached it, she looked up, and the light was red, so she slammed on the brakes, and my head cracked the windshield. The doctor teased her later about that, saying that she wanted me to have an injury on both ends.

My restlessness at the camp meeting was an influence that made Mother decide I needed to learn how to behave in church. She said that she stood on the porch of the house, the first Sunday we were there, which overlooked the town of Magdalena. She could see three steeples, so she knew there were three churches there. She knew one was Catholic. Every town in New Mexico has a Catholic church, and she didn't want to go there. She also thought there would be a Pentecostal church, and she definitely didn't want to go there, so she tried for the other church. There was no name on it, but it was a good church, so that's the church we attended. She said it was about four weeks before she discovered it was Presbyterian. My education was very wearing on both Mother and me. I think she took me outside three times that first Sunday and spanked me. I did learn to sit quietly in church, but it was a hard lesson for both of us.

> *She genuinely loved working with children and was very good at it.*

Before she was there more than a month or so, they had her teaching the children. She genuinely loved working with children and was very good at it. I have an idea that she taught what was in the lesson, but I also know that if she found something that wasn't biblical, she taught the children what was true.

That fall, she taught the school at Rancho Grande. For those who have been fortunate enough to have read the book *Three Angels over Rancho Grande*, you should be familiar with the story of Old Brother Martinez. Mother was hired to teach his grandchildren. His two youngest children, Lucas and Max, were attending an Adventist college in Mexico that year. That was the school year of 1942-43. My brother was seven that year, so she started him in school. She told me later that she should have put him in a class by himself, since he spoke English and that was what the other little children had to learn. It held him back, and he didn't learn like he should have. Since I was only four, turned five, I didn't go to school, but she sat me in the corner and taught me how to crochet. I probably spent some time outside, and I'm sure the other women kept an eye on me, too. That was where Mother saw the difference between a public school education and a church school education and determined that we children would always go to a church school.

It was while we were there that Mother discovered what an asset to the church Ellen White has been. Mother and another family were the only non-Mexican families there, since it consisted of the Martinez grandchildren. Brother Evans worked in the office that year. He had bought the *Testimony Treasures*, then decided he needed the full set of *Testimonies*. Mother, to help him out, bought them from him, and it was while reading them that she discovered how the Lord had used Ellen White to direct the church.

Brother Evans had several children, and he teased them unmercifully. Mother had never been around anyone who teased until she met Daddy, and it had been a real worry to her that he teased us. She said after watching how Brother Evans teased his children and saw that they were not hurt by it (in fact, they were very crazy about him), she became resigned to Daddy teasing us. From what she said, they had argued about it since she was so unaccustomed to that. It didn't stop Daddy, but it did cause conflict between them.

That winter, at Christmas time, we went to San Diego to spend a little time with Daddy, who was still stationed there. He rented a room for us in a private house. There were no hotel rooms available, and motels hadn't been invented at that time. To make the matter worse, Mother had gotten on the wrong train at one of their changes, and we ended up in Los Angeles and had to travel down to San Diego, which made us very late. We arrived there right at midnight. Daddy had met several trains before then, but he had returned to the base, so there we were, in a strange town, no place to stay with two very tired and sleepy children.

She had planned on just staying in the train depot, but they closed shortly after we arrived, so she found herself out on the street with no place to go. I can remember that night. I had on a pair of new boots, and as I walked, they got heavier and heavier. Mother was carrying her suitcase in one hand and had me by the other hand, and I can remember her jerking my hand and saying, "Pick up your feet." She found a policeman and asked him if there was a YWCA nearby. He said yes and showed her where it was. When she got there, they told her it was full. She then asked them if she could stay in the lobby for the night, that she was sure her husband would be there the next day to take care of them. They were very helpful, let her lie down on one of the couches, got blankets for her and us, and we even got some food there the next morning, I think. One of the people called the base and got a message to Daddy, telling him where we were. He was really relieved to know that we had arrived and were all right.

As I said, he had rented a room for us in a private house, but we spent very little time there. Mother told me later that part of the reason is that the man and woman there were constantly arguing, and she didn't want us to hear all that, so we explored the town. We spent at least three days at the San Diego Zoo. I vividly remember the mountain gorillas and the ibexes, I think, who had a little look-out point in their location. We also spent one day in the museum located there. I remember the whale jawbone. It took up two tables and, to a four-year-old, was mammoth.

I don't remember going to church in San Diego, but knowing Mother, I'm sure we did since we were there over at least one Sabbath. By that time, I had learned to behave in church, so that wouldn't have been a problem.

The ride back to Rancho Grande was much better. We stayed on the correct trains, and John and I played with some of the things we had received for Christmas. I remember playing with some toy animals that Mother had gotten at the zoo.

The church at Rancho Grande was conducted in Spanish. One of the sons of old Brother Martinez did the preaching, and it was always in Spanish. Mother said she never did learn to follow the sermons, but she did learn to follow most of the prayers. I did learn to speak Spanish, being a young child, but in the years that followed, I wasn't around anyone who spoke it, and I forgot what I had learned; however, I have been told that I have very good pronunciation.

At the end of the school year, Mother sent John and me back to Magdalena with a mail carrier, and she stayed behind to finish up. When we arrived, Aunt Emily hired a local teenaged girl to come and stay with us. One of the things Aunt Emily asked her to do was heat a number five can (about 7 cups) of honey that had turned to sugar. (In case you don't know, sugar was rationed, so we sweetened with honey, which wasn't rationed). She did the task, but she didn't know to loosen the lid. When it got hot, the lid blew off, and honey went everywhere. Aunt Emily cleaned up what she could, but Mother finished the job when she arrived home a couple of days later. Aunt Emily said she came home that evening and found me licking honey off the wall.

In the summer of 1943, Daddy managed to get transferred to the base at Mojave, California. It was a new base, just being built, so Daddy had to wait until they got the housing built before he could send for us. He was working as an MP (miliary police), guarding the prisoners. Mother and Aunt Emily packed up all our things, including Mother's sewing machine and her linens. We traveled by train, and the first part of the trip was really hot as we went across Arizona. That evening, at Phoenix, I think, we changed trains into one that was air conditioned. By this time, it was evening, and the AC was going full blast. We almost froze.

Daddy met us at the train depot in a jeep and told Mother, "I was at the house today. There is nothing in it but the beds."

Mother said she didn't care. She said, "Just get us somewhere so we can lie down." So, we ended the night in our new home without covers or pillows. Within two to three days, they brought the furniture, and it was a very comfortable apartment. The kitchen was actually part of the living room, so Mother made a long curtain out of denim to separate them. Mother said those were good years. The only problem they had was that Daddy started drinking. He would go to the NCO (non-commissioned officer) club with his buddies and have a glass of beer most days, and this really bothered Mother. Granddad never drank, so Mother wasn't used to being around that.

The housing was a four-apartment building, and we had the middle apartment. Next door to us was a family with a son who was a young teenager. John was excited because we hadn't ever lived where there were other children with whom to play, but here was a boy who was several years older and kind enough to let John follow after him, at least part of the time. Incidentally, on the other side of us was a family who had a little boy who was about the same number of years younger, who was thrilled when John would let him tag along. Mother said it was interesting to watch how it played out. John would be upset when the older boy was too busy to play with him, but he wouldn't always play with the younger boy, who would be hurt.

The house was furnished with two double beds. Although we were young, Mother didn't like the idea of John and me sleeping together. She soon discovered that the one room apartments were furnished with twin beds, so she made arrangements with a newly married couple to change our double bed for their two twins, which was approved by both parties.

We also went to church there; I think it was a Christian church. As usual, it wasn't long until they had Mother teaching the children. Of course, we kept the Sabbath at home, but it was nice to have Christian friends, and Mother received a real blessing from being part of that church, as did we children. During all this time, Mother had remained a member of the Texaco Conference Church, sending in her tithe and offerings as she got them. She didn't join a local church until we moved to Albuquerque at the end of the war.

Sometime after we moved to Mojave, I don't remember just when, we attended a large gathering of Adventists. How Mother knew about it, I have no idea, but if I remember correctly, it was held in Glendale. The things I remember about it was the ride to it on a bus, and I think the program included a large choir on Sabbath afternoon. The members were black, and I suspect it was several churches combined because I do remember that they filled the stage. They sang negro spirituals. I had never heard them before, and I still remember their singing, acapella. The songs that impressed me the most were "Rock-a-My Soul in the Bosom of Abraham" and "Swing Low, Sweet Chariot." This was the only time while we were there that Mother had any contact with other Adventists that I can remember.

Mojave is right on the edge of the desert, and it gets very hot there in the summer, but the houses were air conditioned, and it wasn't bad. Daddy told me about looking at a thermometer and it reading 132 degrees. The men were encouraged to drink a lot of water and beside every water fountain was a box of salt tablets. To the west of us were the Tehachapi Mountains, but the east was strictly desert. Other than a few Joshua trees, nothing grew there. There was a fence and guards to keep us in, and I suppose, others out. On Sabbath, she would often take us out on the desert, and we pretended we were the children of Israel, wandering in the desert. She usually had to argue with the guard, but when he would see that she had water along and was determined, we were always allowed to go.

Among other things, the base had a large swimming pool. It was discovered shortly after the war began that almost as many men died from drowning as were killed when they landed on the islands, so every man had to learn to swim before he was sent overseas. Remember, the Marines are part of the Navy, so they were on board ships. There were no diving boards. The deep end was rigged like a ship, and the shallow end was about chest high in an adult. The mornings were used for instructing the men, but the pool was open for the dependents to use in the afternoons. That's where I learned to swim. They had canvas pillows they gave to us children to keep us afloat, and as far as I know, none of us drowned. The water there came from a large pipeline that supplied Los Angeles, I think, from Lake Tahoe. Since it was a military installation, they had priority. Mother said the pipe was so large that a truck could be driven through it. There was never a shortage of water there, but it wasn't used for gardening, just household use.

John started the second grade. Mother went in and talked to the teacher and explained the situation to her, that she felt John hadn't had a very good opportunity the year before. The teacher was very understanding and said she would do what she could to help John. When she tested him, he was put into the next to the lowest group in her room. However, as the year progressed, he moved up until, at the end of the year, he was in the top group.

I stayed home that year, but the next year I went to kindergarten. I was six then, and they wanted to start me in the first grade, but Mother kept me back, and it was a good thing she did. I remember my teacher well; her name was Mrs. Black, and she walked with a limp. She was very patient with us, and I really loved her. The school was in town, and we rode to and from on the base bus. It was driven by a young Marine, and one day, with the encouragement of the kids, he went really fast over the bumps. I think they were street crossings, but I do remember sailing through the air and landing in the seat behind me. I'm not the only one that did some sailing that day, so he told us that he couldn't do that anymore. As far as I know, none of us were hurt, but that was not really a safe thing to do.

It was there that Mother really started making money with her sewing. The fatigue uniforms didn't have hip pockets, and most of the men wanted them, so she had a lively business. Because of that, when we left California at the end of the war, they had a very good savings account.

Shortly after we arrived, Mother became pregnant with Anna. Since Daddy was military, she went to the base doctor. Part of the problem with that was that she often saw a different doctor. The one she had the longest time was a very good doctor and helped her through the first part of her pregnancy. As I mentioned before, she had at least two miscarriages and didn't want to lose this baby. He put her on thyroid medication and extra vitamins, and she did manage to carry Anna. After about the middle of her pregnancy, however, he left and from then on it was one doctor after another. She had a new doctor the night that Anna was born. He was a gynecologist who had been sent there because the base commander's wife was pregnant. He had been a doctor to some of the Hollywood stars, and she said he bragged about that. He delivered Anna with high forceps and tore mother up very badly. She said she had a heavy discharge for several months afterward, and as she put it, she "spent a lot of time in the knee-chest position." More about this later.

It was also there that Mother had her teeth pulled and received her first set of dentures. Her mother hadn't liked milk, and every one of her children, by the time they were forty, had dentures. Mother started losing teeth by the time she was in her late teens and had lost most of her back teeth by the time she was married. The dentist took an impression of her front teeth and had her plate made with the same look, which really pleased mother. She had what she called "peg teeth," which were two small teeth at the side. When we moved back to Albuquerque and she saw the people there who had known her before we went to California, most of them didn't realize she had dentures. She used those teeth for about twenty-five years; that dentist had given her a really good pair. He pulled the rest of her back teeth and let the gums heal. Then he pulled the front teeth and put in the plates that day. She went back the next morning, and he took them out, cleaned them, and put them back in. She never went without teeth from that day on. All her life she slept with them and would remove them only for cleaning. While her mouth was so sore, she learned to eat an apple by scraping it with a spoon. After Anna was born, she also gave her fresh apple that way.

I have mentioned earlier about what a tease Daddy was. He really enjoyed teasing, and we children were often the ones he picked on, especially me. She told me about one incident. I do remember some of this, but it took her recounting the whole thing to bring it back to my memory. Mother always had some kind of dessert for dinner, served at noon. Daddy started bringing home a candy bar, and I would trade him my dessert for the candy bar. This went on for probably a week or more, until I got used to doing it. Then one day he indicated that he didn't have the candy bar but still wanted my desert. After he had persuaded me that I could have the candy bar later, probably that evening, he ate my dessert, then pulled the candy bar out of his pocket and told Mother to give it to me that evening. Of course, I set up a howl and, I think, finally got the candy bar. Later, Mother accused him of lying to me, and he assured her that he hadn't. She said she thought over very carefully what he had said, and he hadn't actually said he didn't have the candy bar. He had just let me think that.

I do remember this. One day Daddy asked me to get him a drink of water. When I took it to him, the water was warm, so he sent me back to get some cold water. Being his daughter, I saw a chance to tease him, so I filled it with hot water and didn't realize that the hot water had bubbles in it, so when I walked around the curtain, he could see that it was hot. He told me to get cold water. When I asked him how he knew it wasn't cold, he pointed out the bubbles in it. I went back, dumped out the water, but again filled it with hot water. However, I stood there until the bubbles had all dissipated, then carried it to him. It wasn't until he took hold of the glass that he realized it was hot. After that, I finally did get him the cold water. He had gotten somewhat cross with me, but Mother reminded him that he liked to tease us, and he needed to let us tease him, so he said no more. Mother always said that I was the most like him of all the children.

As I said, Daddy's job was guarding the prisoners, none of whom were really serious offenders. He would take them out every day to let them work and take them back in the evening to spend the night in the jail. He came home for lunch/dinner, so I am assuming they ate with the other men in the mess hall. I'm not sure how it came about, but Daddy asked Mother what she thought of letting one of the prisoners come stay with us over the weekend and spend some time with his wife, who would be at our house. She agreed, though rather reluctantly, and so Daddy went to his commanding officer to get the OK. Approval was given, with the stipulation that Daddy have a gun in the house, why I don't know. Either that day or the next, the sergeant came to the house to leave the gun. Mother wasn't in favor of it being there and asked him to at least unload it, so if one of us children got ahold of it, we couldn't fire it. He sat down at the table to unload it, with both John and me watching very closely. Apparently, I had crowded in closer, because the gun went off, and I lost some of my bangs. The bullet, after clipping my hair, went through two walls before going into the ceiling in one of the bedrooms. Daddy learned about it when the sergeant walked up to Daddy and told him that he had almost killed his little girl. Daddy said the man was still shaking over it. They didn't insist on Daddy keeping a gun there after that.

The experiment worked out well. The men were grateful for the chance to spend a weekend with their wives, and Mother made some good friends over this. However, the last woman who came wasn't the kind of person Mother wanted us children around. She stayed several weeks, and Mother almost had to throw her out. She wasn't clean, and Mother discovered later that she and the man weren't even married. One thing that really upset Mother was when she, Mother, discovered the woman had brought bedbugs with her. It didn't take her long to get rid of them. She told me, later, that "It isn't a disgrace to get bedbugs, but it is to keep them." After that, even Daddy refused to let anyone come again.

When it became obvious that Mother was pregnant, the ladies of the church gave her a shower. I can remember it because I couldn't understand why Mother was getting so many things, and I got nothing. (I told you I was a brat.) One dear, sweet sister told me not to worry because that next Sunday she would have something for me, and she brought me a very nice doll made from a sock. I really loved that doll and kept it for many years.

Anna was born in August, so she was about four months old that Christmas. The church put on a Christmas pageant, and Anna was the baby Jesus. She was always a happy baby and during the play was laying in the "manger," cooing. She could be heard all over the auditorium. On Sundays, Mother would feed her, then take her into the pastor's house and lay her on the bed during the sermon.

One Sunday, one of the families asked Mother if John and I could go home with them, so Mother got on the bus without any of her children. Daddy was on the bus, and his first question was "Where are the kids?" Mother said we had gone home with another family. He said, "The baby, too?" She had completely forgotten Anna. She jumped off the bus and rushed to the pastor's house to find the pastor and his wife enjoying their time with Anna. When Mother explained, they laughed and said that if she wanted to leave Anna with them, they wouldn't object.

The base held classes for the new mothers, and Mother attended. One of the things they were told was to remember they were on the desert. "If you are warm, so is your baby" was one of the things they were told. "Don't try to keep them bundled up, that can cause real problems." So, especially during the hot weather, Anna wore only a diaper. We got our mail at the post office, and Mother said that one day, she parked Anna's carriage outside while she went in to get the mail. It happened to be in front of the window, so Mother saw one of the ladies stop, look in at the sleeping baby, then pick up the receiving blanket Mother had folded at the foot of the carriage, gently cover Anna with it, then move on. When she finished inside, she removed the blanket, folded it, and placed it at the foot of the baby carriage. They were also advised to offer the babies water frequently, and Anna drank a lot of water. She seemed to need it, as did we all.

There are two things I vividly remember happening while we were living in Mojave. I came in one day and found Mother kneeling by the couch. She was praying, and I asked what was wrong. She said she had just heard that President Roosevelt had died. She said she was praying for the new president, Harry Truman. The other thing I remember was being called in and hurriedly being dressed in my best clothes. I asked Mother where we were going. She said that it had just been announced that the war was over, and we were going to the chapel to pray. Imagine her amazement when she discovered that everyone wasn't running to the chapel, but to the NCO club for free beer.

It was shortly after that that Daddy was discharged from the Marines. He left almost immediately to return to his job with the Veterans Hospital in Albuquerque. Mother stayed to get things ready to ship home, then we went to San Francisco to stay with Aunt Emily until her husband, Uncle Cotton, arrived.

Aunt Emily had met Cotton (probably a nickname) Hogsett while she was working at Magdalena. He owned a ranch in southwest New Mexico, located between the towns of Pie Town and Quemado. He wasn't a Christian, but from what I understand, they were happy together. He loved her and treated her well. During the war he was a gunner on one of the ships in the Pacific and sailed in about two weeks after we got there. She had an apartment, and it was about two blocks from the bay shore. John and I went down to watch the ocean and play there. It wasn't a sandy beach, just some rocks, as I remember. We could sit on the rocks and watch the ships go by, and there were a lot of ships, too. While there, we rode on one of the ferries across the bay. I'm not sure where we were going, but we did enjoy it.

The other thing I remember about San Francisco is the steep sidewalks, with steps in them. There wasn't much running done because it was too hard to run up the stairs. Mother talked about the large basement where the ladies were able to dry their washing. (No dryers then.) Each lady had her day to wash and dry her clothes. Because of the climate there, drying the clothes outside could be a problem.

We did go to church there. The closest one was a black church. Mother said it was interesting to watch the little black children come and touch Anna, who was very pale compared to them and had cotton white hair.

John and I hadn't met Uncle Cotton before, but it didn't take him long to earn our affection. He was big and jolly and loved to play with us. He seemed to understand me, and that was a real boost to my morale. He and I made an agreement. While we were together, he would wake me up. I would then get up and turn on the fire under the coffee pot, so when he got up, the coffee would be perked. He woke me up by tying a string to my big toe, and he would pull it when he woke up, which woke me up. We did this the whole time we were with them, and it was a real pleasure to me, and he really enjoyed it, too, or seemed to.

We all left there shortly after he arrived and drove in their car up to Portland, Oregon, where Granddad was working in the shipyards. On the way up, since we were driving through northern California, we stopped and saw some of the national parks. I remember seeing the TALL redwoods. We spent some time among them, but as I was only seven, I don't remember very much about them. Granddad actually was the maintenance man for the housing project that had been built to house the men and women who built the ships. We were there two weeks, and we had a very good time.

The main thing I remember about Portland was the donut machine. It squeezed out a circle of dough into a bucket of hot grease that had little dividers that went around. At the halfway point, a paddle turned the dough over, and when it came out, it was cooked. John and I stood and watched it for some time when Granddad took us to see it. I'm sure he bought us a donut that had just been made.

While we were there, we crossed the Columbia River and went up into Washington state. None of us had ever been there before, so Uncle Cotton was as interested in going as were the rest of us. I'm sure Granddad went with us. The car must have been crowded with four adults and three children. If I remember correctly, I sat in the front with Granddad and Uncle Cotton, while the others sat in the back. I was always prone to motion sickness and did better in the front seat.

I'm not sure how long the ride to Albuquerque took. I know we stayed in a motel several nights. Mother had made a night gown-bed jacket set that she was really proud of and accidentally left the bed jacket at one of the motels. She said she tried to get it back, even tried to write to them, but it wasn't returned. We stopped at Shiprock, New Mexico. I remember seeing the big rock for which it was named (which does look somewhat like a ship) and Aunt Emily telling me that the Indians said it was what had brought them to North America. I also remember the first view I had of Albuquerque. We came in on Route 66, traveling east. This was in the summer of 1945, and it was dry and hot traveling across the desert. We topped the hills and looked down on the Rio Grande valley where there were trees and greenery. What a wonderful sight after the long, hot road we had traveled.

RETURN TO ALBUQUERQUE

We went to Uncle Billy's home, since the place Daddy had found for us wasn't finished. After the war, there was a great shortage of houses. Many of the men were returning home with brides from the countries where they had been stationed. The whole country had put their entire efforts into the war, so many of the things that would have normally been done were neglected, and housing was one of them. When Daddy had returned to Albuquerque, he started looking for some kind of house for us. He finally found where two houses were being built. He put down two months' rent on one of them and went by every week or two to see that someone else had not rented it out from under him. I'm not sure how long we stayed with Uncle Billy and Aunt Monnie, but it was several weeks.

The day we arrived, Aunt Monnie came home from the hospital with her youngest son, little John E. (John is a very prevalent name in our family.) She didn't have some of the supplies she needed, so Mother was forced to drive to the drug store to get them. Remember, it had been seven or eight years since she had driven, and she was never a good driver. She said later that she was really nervous. However, she did it and returned with the things that were needed. Aunt Emily and Uncle Cotton had already left. They had another five to six hours of driving to reach his ranch in southwestern New Mexico.

> *I'm not sure how Mother paid for our schooling in those years, probably from her savings, but she was determined to have us in church school.*

We must have arrived in the month of September because my brother John and I started school. I was in the first grade, and he was in the third. We started in the public school, but we only went there until Mother could arrange for us to attend church school. Our teacher was Miss Alexander, and the school was an old building. The school building and the church were sold during the next school year, with the provision that we were allowed to continue using the school until the school year was finished. The new church was built on the corner of Ash and Coal Street. I'm not sure how Mother paid for our schooling in those years, probably from her savings, but she was determined to have us in church school.

When we moved into the house, we had very little furniture. The housing at Mojave was furnished. So, one of the first things Mother and Daddy had to do was get some furniture. I do remember sleeping in a packing crate until they got us bunkbeds. They slept on the rollaway bed they had, and Anna slept in a dresser drawer. I don't remember where John slept. They did get Anna's crib put up, at the foot of their bed, with the bunkbeds across from their bed. The dresser was at the foot of the bunkbeds. The door to the bathroom was at the head of the bunkbeds.

The house was very tiny. It was comprised of three rooms, each nine by nine feet. The first room was the living room, the kitchen was next, and the bedroom was right behind it, all three in a row, with the bathroom built on the west side, containing a sink and a toilet. Mother had to do some real arranging to get us all placed. The other house opposite was exactly the same, except its bathroom was on the east side, so there was a narrow passage between the two houses. I don't usually remember numbers, but I do remember the address of that house: 808 Anderson. The street in front wasn't paved, and we had to walk several blocks to the bus stop. I remember John helping Mother by pulling Anna's baby carriage through the sand while Mother pushed.

My memories of that time are somewhat vague. I do know it was in the poorer part of town, and our neighbors were all Mexican. There was a water hydrant outside, and I remember watching the neighbor lady each morning washing the chili meat out of the pods and wondering how she made it. I also remember being in their house and looking at a song book they had.

They were trying to sing "Old Black Joe," and getting it very wrong, so I took the book and sang it for them. They all commented on what a pretty voice I had. I also remember when they killed a goat. They hung it up by its back legs and cut its throat. I watched it kick until it stopped. I think I was crying; I know I wasn't happy about it. One thing that really amazed me was their catching the blood to make blood pudding.

Another memory is that we always went to prayer meeting, and coming home one Wednesday evening, we passed a church where there was a lot of noise coming from the basement. John and I ran over to look in the basement windows and were shocked to see people dancing in there. We both went running back to Mother, telling her what we had seen. She had the job of trying to make us understand that not all people believed as we did.

One other thing I remember while living there was that Uncle Anderson, Daddy's brother, came into Albuquerque with a badly infected hand. He was living at our place in the Estancia valley, and while working on a tractor, he had driven a screwdriver into the place between his thumb and fingers. He had neglected it until he had red streaks going up his arm. He stayed with us for several days while Mother soaked his hand in Epsom salt water. I remember looking at it and seeing the "white stuff" coming out. He told me it was the infection.

Meanwhile, Daddy was looking for a place to buy. I'm not sure how he heard about the place they bought, but the story goes that a young man was getting married and couldn't find an available home, so he went to the Estancia valley and got one of the abandoned houses there, had it moved into Albuquerque, and sat it on a lot. It had no plumbing, wiring, or any modern conveniences at all. Between the living room and the kitchen there was a large, concrete flue that served both rooms, and it broke when it was moved and knocked down the ceiling in two rooms. When he took his bride-to-be to look at the home, which he was providing for her, she had the good sense to quit him cold, so he had this house and no bride. He sold it to Daddy for $1,200 dollars. It was on one lot from the corner, so they also bought the lot on either side of them so they wouldn't have close neighbors. This was located outside the city limits, on South Louisiana Street, four blocks south of Central, which is the old Route 66.

Before we could move into it, Daddy had to repair the ceiling in the two rooms and do some other work on it. It was probably two to three months before he could get it livable. I remember going with him one day to "help" him. It was hot weather, and we stopped and ate lunch at a cafe that had AC.

The outside walls of the house were 12" x 12" boards that had been staggered, and a 1" x 4" placed over the outside seam. The inside walls were simply a 1" x 12" and then they had been papered over them. There was only one window in each room, so one of the first things Daddy had to do was put in more windows. This was a problem, since building supplies were really short, and he could only buy two window casements at a time, but as he told me later, that was all he could afford, anyway.

The house consisted of four rooms: the living room in front, which was the southwest room, two bedrooms to the back and to the side, and the kitchen at the northeast side of the building. In order to go from the kitchen to the living room, it was necessary to go through either one or the other of the bedrooms. Mother took the southeast bedroom for the kitchen, so it was next to the living room. She had Daddy close the door to the northwest bedroom and make the former kitchen into three tiny rooms, two bedrooms and a bathroom. There was a hall between them and the bigger bedroom, on the west side, which was theirs. My room was the northmost room, and there was a spot of oil in the doorway where someone in the past had set the milk separator that had dripped oil. Mother had to scrub it with lye every month or so for several months until she finally got all the oil out of the wood. Next was the room for John, and then there was the bathroom. Later, the partition between the two bedrooms was removed, making a fair-sized bedroom.

Daddy cut a door from the kitchen into the hall and closed up all the other inside doors. He cut a door to the outside on the east side of the kitchen and part of the broken chimney was the steps into the house. As I said, there were no modern conveniences built into the house, including water. Until they got the pipes laid to bring water to the house, we carried water from our neighbor's house to the north of us. They had an outside faucet that stood several feet above ground, and we could go there with our buckets and carry water home. Mother took some number five honey buckets for John and me to haul water in.

By this time, Anna was two years old and was wanting to help, too, so Mother took a sixteen ounce can and put a bail on it for her to carry water in. As we approached the back door, we would yell, "Open the door," and Mother would hold it open for us.

At first, Anna yelled, what Daddy said "as "Opidoppidy," but when he got to teasing her about it, she would simply yell, "Door," so Mother could let her in. Mother cooked with a coal oil stove and used some kind of contraption as an oven. It could be set on one of the burners. We used coal oil lamps and had a coal stove in the living room for heat. Before we could move in, Daddy built an outhouse at the back of the lot, so we truly had four rooms and a path.

I don't remember the move, but it had to have been about the time school started. I do remember traveling on the city bus to school and the walk home from the bus stop. John and I were small children. This was our second year in Albuquerque, so he had to have been eleven that year, which was old enough to travel on the bus and to make sure I was with him. We had to change buses downtown, so he had to make sure we got on the right bus.

That year, at Christmas time, we went into Penney's to look at the Christmas toys. All at once, he grabbed my hand and said, "Hurry, it's almost time for the bus." The toy department was on the second floor, so we had to go down the stairs, and somehow, I fell down the last few of them. He was ahead of me but must have heard the *thump* as I landed at the bottom. He turned and said, "Come on! We'll miss the bus."

My answer was a tearful wail, "I can't," *boohoo*.

"Come on," he insisted, but it wasn't any use, I just couldn't walk on my ankle. As I sat there crying, with him trying to get me up, one of the store employees came, picked me up, and walked out with me with John in hot pursuit. He took me to a doctor's office where the doctor wrapped my ankle with an ace wrap. He told us that I had a badly sprained ankle and to stay off it for several days. Then the man from Penney's put us in a taxicab and sent us home. Meanwhile, Mother was wondering why we hadn't arrived home. It was past time for us to be there. You can imagine her surprise when a taxicab drove up, and the driver got out and carried me into the house. She said later that her first thought was "What have those children been up to now?" The driver explained that he had already been paid, so she didn't have to pay him and that I was to stay off my ankle until it was better.

When Daddy got home and was told what had happened, his only comment was, "They did that so we wouldn't sue them."

Mother's answer was, "I don't see how we could, since they had no business being in there in the first place." (They weren't the suing kind.)

My only other real memory of that school year was the play we put on for the end of the year. It was about how different people responded to the cross they were given. I don't think I had a part in it, but I do remember the older children practicing their parts. Each person had a different size cross, some very small, others bigger. The biggest cross was given to a girl name Tiny Archuleta, who was the daughter of the Spanish pastor. It was about as tall as she was.

With each cross there was a hymn, as the person finally accepted the responsibility of keeping it, and I remember her singing, "I am Coming to the Cross." She had a lovely voice, which may have been part of the reason she was chosen for that part.

Springtime in Albuquerque was always windy, especially up on the higher elevations. Since there were no natural trees around, the wind usually picked up some dust and that could include some small rocks. John and I had four blocks to walk after we got off the bus, and walking in the wind could be difficult. I can remember squatting down and covering my head with my arms when the really strong gusts hit us, so I wouldn't be blown over.

We were outside the city limits, in fact there was nothing much between us and the town but open prairie where a lot of tumble weeds grew. That and "goat heads" were the only things that grew without cultivation. Mother put in a garden the next summer, and it did well, but she never did get tomatoes to grow there. The wind was too much for them.

As usual, Mother was sewing to earn money. Remember, she had our school bill to pay, so she did it by sewing. Louisiana Street was one of the entrances to Sandia Base and was fairly busy. I'm not sure how she got her customers, but when we got home from school, she was usually sewing.

Daddy was working the evening shift at the Veterans Hospital, from 4 p.m. to 12 a.m., so it was just us every evening. It was about the same time that Daddy signed up for schooling under the GI bill. His choice was a course in cabinet making. He did it for several reasons, mostly, I think, because he was paid while going to school, but it meant he was in school all morning and worked in the evenings. It took him two years to complete the course, but he really enjoyed working with wood, and when he was finished, he started working at making furniture on the side. While still at the school, he made the bedroom set that he and Mother used for the rest of their lives and is in my bedroom now. He eventually earned some money by making things for others and made several really nice pieces of furniture for the family, including a desk out of Philippine mahogany. One problem with the things he made was that they were well-made and very heavy. He made a coffee table for his sister, Aunt Ruby, that was so heavy she couldn't move it.

By that next summer, we had water in the house. Daddy had dug a cesspool, so we had an indoor toilet and a natural gas stove. Daddy found an old cook stove that had been thrown out. It had four burners and an oven, but the bottom of the oven was rusted out, so mother put a piece of asbestos in it, and it worked very well. It had additional pieces of metal, like wings, on each side that were detachable, and on one of them was the date 1912. We assumed that was when it was made. It was a big improvement over the coal oil stove she had been using, and she was very thankful for the oven. She started baking bread again, and Daddy was happy that he could have his corn bread every day. We also had a gas refrigerator. Our heat was a little gas stove in the front room that heated that room adequately, and the gas burners kept the kitchen warm. If I remember correctly, it was about that same time that the house was wired for electricity. We were really getting modern living conveniences. Daddy had gotten the windows in, so we had windows in every room and had put plaster board inside to cover the walls.

It was that year, in the winter of 1947-48, that the church was sold, and the new building was built on the corner of Lead and Ash. Since the school building had been sold also, they planned on using the church basement for the school room. The building didn't go up as rapidly as it was thought it would, so we didn't start school until very late that year. In fact, in order to get in the required number of days, we had to go to school on several Sundays. Since we rode the bus, we used tokens, worth a nickel, and the bus driver was very reluctant to allow us to use them on a Sunday, since it was unusual for children to be going to school on the weekend. The school was on one side of the building, and the other side was used for the sanctuary until they got the roof on, the inside plastered, and the pews installed.

That was also the year that Albuquerque had several blizzards. To put it mildly, our house wasn't built for that kind of weather. To make matters worse, the gas line wasn't adequate to supply all the businesses going up Central Street and the houses that were being built to the east. When the storms hit, the gas pressure decreased until the flames were just tiny buds, producing almost no heat. The only way to keep warm was to stay in bed. Daddy must have been at the hospital, so he didn't come home during the blizzards. I can remember staying in bed with Mother, John, and Anna. She read to us, and we played under the covers.

When the second blizzard hit, Uncle Bill came and got us and took us to his home, where we stayed until the blizzard was over. When we returned home, Mother said she took two washtubs of snow out of my room alone. That next spring Daddy put siding on the outside, to make the house more weatherproof. It was gray and had a rock pattern. Later, he contracted with a company to apply another kind of siding, over the rock one, that made the house really warm. The gas company also put in a larger pipe that next spring, so we never had that problem again.

It may have been when the siding was put on the house that John and I decided to get up on the roof. There had to have been a ladder there or else we couldn't have gotten up there. The roof was very steep, so walking on it was dangerous, and to make it even worse, we decided to take Anna with us. She was maybe three years old currently. John was cautious enough to put a rope around her middle, and he had ahold of the other end, but it was decidedly not a safe thing to do. We had been up there for about ten minutes or so when Mother came out to see what was going on. She yelled something at us. I didn't understand what she said, but John said she had told us to get down, right now, then she turned and went back inside. Many years later I asked her why she had gone back inside, and her reply was, "I couldn't stand the thought of watching my baby fall to her death." When we got back inside, we were severely told that if we wanted to get up on the roof, we could do it but never, under any circumstances, were we to take Anna up there again.

John and I did go back up on the roof from time to time. The government was digging into the mountain, building Manzano Base, which was, we were told, a place where they were going to store atomic bombs. From the roof, we could see some of the activity along the mountainside. From what we were told later, the men who were working on the construction were carried there in busses that had the windows blacked out, so they were unable to see where they were going. Only the driver knew how to get there. It was all very hush-hush.

I mentioned earlier that Mother had joined the Episcopal church when she was living in Albuquerque as a teenager. By that time, Grandmother had become a follower of Sister Aimee McPherson, who was one of the first Pentecostal evangelists. Mother said she could never understand what they were teaching. It didn't make sense to her, and she liked the reverence in the Episcopal church. After she became an Adventist, she studied both the Bible and Sister White's writings in an attempt to really understand how to serve the Lord with all her heart. She stopped believing in the pagan holidays of Easter and Christmas, like others did. We still hunted Easter eggs and got presents at Christmas, but she certainly didn't believe in going into debt for gifts.

We always got a new summer outfit for thirteenth Sabbath in the spring. At that time, thirteenth Sabbath was a big deal in the church. The children came before the Sabbath School and, among other things, repeated all the memory verses they had learned that quarter. We children always had three sets of clothes: our Sabbath clothes, our school clothes, and the clothes we played in. Under no circumstances did we wear our Sabbath clothes for anything but going to church. We girls even had special underwear for the Sabbath. I remember Mother telling me when I was grown that before she wore a new dress, she dedicated it to the Lord. If it was really nice, she wore it to church. If it was a regular house dress, she wore it to prayer meeting. That was how much she respected the Lord.

I'm also going to talk about Mother's hair. She was twenty-eight when I was born, but already at that time, she had a lot of gray in her hair. This is an inherited tendency in our family. I can never remember her hair being anything but gray. After she joined the church, she never cut it again. When she was young, the style was the bob, and that's how she wore it until she accepted the Adventist faith. She was shown the council given by Paul in 1 Corinthians 11, and she never cut it again. It was very thick, and she wore it with a roll on the back of her head. She loved to have her hair combed or brushed. I was quite young when I discovered that one way to get on her good side, after some of my naughtiness, was to offer to brush or comb her hair. She would sit down in a chair, and I would comb it for her for several minutes. It almost always put her in a good mood, and we both enjoyed it. However, one time I wound the comb up in her hair, and if I remember correctly, took it almost to her head. When I tried to unwind it, of course, it didn't happen. That's when she discovered what I had done. I'm not sure how she managed to unwind it, but it was some time before she let me comb her hair again.

It was about this time that the Glovers moved in next door. Their house was directly north of us. There was a house to the south of us across Bell Street, but we were never friendly with that family. However, the Glovers had two girls, Jewell and Sherill. Jewell was a month older than I was, and Sherill was two years younger. We were the only children in that neighborhood for several years, so we were quite close. Mother and Mrs. Glover were good friends. Daddy and Mr. Glover enjoyed each other's company but were never real buddies.

It was after they had all become friends that Mother pulled a real joke on the men. At that time, Mrs. Glover's brother was staying with them. The men were playing cards, and Mother and Mrs. Glover were having a nice visit when someone decided to make some fudge. Mother had a very good recipe that she was proud of, so she made the fudge. However, before she poured it into the pans to cool, she reserved a small portion and loaded it with cayenne pepper. She baited her trap well by giving the men a plate of the good candy, which they all enjoyed, then she put another plate on the table where they were sitting, with three pieces of the doctored candy. The other two men grabbed a piece, but Daddy didn't since there were only three pieces, and he was, as Mother put it, "too much of a gentleman to take the last piece." They each took a big bite then immediately stood up and headed to the kitchen for some water to drink to get the hot pepper out of their mouths. Mother was never the teaser that Daddy was, but she could, at times, get one over on Daddy.

> *Mother was never the teaser that Daddy was, but she could, at times, get one over on Daddy.*

It must have been the summer of 1947 that Aunt Emily and Uncle Cotton had us come down for part of the summer. The "us" included John, my cousin Larry, and myself. I do know that Anna wasn't included. Larry's brother, Tommy, who was two years younger than Larry, also did not come. As I said before, they lived on a ranch in southwest New Mexico. I do remember that Uncle Bill and Aunt Monnie drove us down there. They explained later that it was cheaper for them to drive us than to pay for the bus fare for three fairly small children, although John was probably ten or eleven and a very responsible boy; he would have been able to handle us.

We were there a month, I think, and enjoyed ourselves very much. Aunt Emily was in bed part of the time. She and Uncle Cotton wanted a family, but she had problems getting pregnant and had to be given some kind of medication by injection, and then had problems carrying the baby. She lost a baby while we were there, so she was in bed part of the time. I don't remember helping her much, but when we returned, Grandad got me a bicycle because I had been such a help to her. I do remember going out with the boys and picking wildflowers and bringing them to her, which I strongly suspect now that she dumped in the trash when we left her room. We had a wonderful time, roaming out in the fresh air and in the hills. I also remember climbing the windmill and playing up there.

That fall, sometime after school started, Aunt Emily again became pregnant, but she hadn't been given the shot this time, so the doctor wasn't expecting it. She had an ectopic pregnancy, which caused the fallopian tube to rupture. Uncle Cotton brought her to Albuquerque for the needed surgery, but it was on a weekend, and there was no anesthetist available, so the doctor administered the anesthesia himself. Grandad said he gave her too much and burned up her brain. Now whether that is what happened, we have no way of knowing, but she never regained consciousness. She lived for about ten more days, and Mother said that she, Grandmother, and the rest of the family, including Uncle Bill, Aunt Monnie, and Aunt Mary, prayed very earnestly that she be laid to rest if she couldn't be restored to what she was before.

I remember her funeral well. They had a service in Albuquerque, but the burial was in a cemetery close to their home. I don't remember more than a grave-side service there, but I do remember how the people there talked about her, how they loved and respected her. She had moved there at the end of the war and apparently had made some close friends in that length of time. They talked about her walk with God and what an inspiration she had been to them.

This was the first death in the family since Mother was a girl, and she really took it hard. She and Aunt Emily had always been very close. Aunt Emily was the only one of the family who was willing to even listen to what Mother believed. She had attended school at Keene and was a baptized member of the church, but over the years, she had drifted away. However, not too long before her death, she had had once again turned to the Lord and was reading her Bible again. She told Mother that she had regretted neglecting the Lord and was truly seeking to turn to Him. Mother told me, years later, that it was the one consolation in her death, that there was a good possibility that she had returned to the Lord and would be among those who were waiting for His return. I have wondered since if John and I had been instrumental in reminding her of God's love.

If I remember correctly, we went to school for two years at the church building on Ash Street. It was there that John was hit in the mouth with a baseball bat and broke his two front teeth. Unfortunately, Mother and Daddy didn't know to take him to a dentist, so he eventually had to have them pulled, and he got a partial plate. What I remember the most about that was how upset I was over it. I really didn't realize how much I loved him until he was hurt.

Our teacher for those two years was Miss Urbish. One day I heard her singing in a different language, and I asked her what language it was. She said it was Czech. I don't know if she was an immigrant or her parents were, but it made an impression on me, hearing her singing a hymn in a different language.

Soon after we moved into the house on the hill, we took a trip to visit Aunt Ruby and Uncle Andrew in Mineral Wells, Texas. Uncle Anderson was staying with us by that time, and he had a Nash. It was a very good car, so that's what we traveled in. Anna was still a baby, and none of Daddy's family had seen her. Besides, it had been several years since he had seen them, and he wanted to show off his children, especially Anna, who was a very pretty, happy baby. I remember that trip well. We had a wonderful time. Uncle Andrew was a good host, and Aunt Ruby was so happy to have all of us there. They had never been able to have children, so they were very good to all the nephews and nieces.

We visited some of the other relatives that lived in the nearby towns. We even went to see their mother's grave in Cisco, but what I remember the most was our trip to the Red River, which separates Oklahoma and Texas. While there, John and I played in the water, and Daddy killed an armadillo. We were taken to the Crazy Water Hotel later and given a glass of the mineral water, and we did drink it, but it wasn't very tasty to me.

During the summer of 1947, Mother decided to send John and me to junior camp. That year, it was held in the Sandia Mountains, just above Albuquerque, so there wasn't any charge to get the campers there. We were told we were going if we hoed the weeds out of the yard. Our yard was fairly large, as it consisted of three lots. I was given the southern part to hoe, and John had the north part, and I really think he had the larger part. He promptly started and, in a few days, had his half of the yard looking very nice, but I did more crying than hoeing. So, when time for junior camp came, guess who got to stay home and who got to go and have a good time. I remember Grandmother coming out one day during this time and trying to get me to work. Her method was to pull the weeds, and in just a few minutes, she had almost a yard clear, but I found that bending over was harder than using the hoe, so I didn't really benefit from her demonstration.

However, the next year, we had to earn the money to go to junior camp. Mother got 200 copies of *Life and Health* (now known as *Vibrant Life*), and we went out to sell them. If I remember correctly, they were twenty-five cents apiece. We got up early, hoed until about 10:00 a.m., then came in, changed clothes, and went out to sell our magazines. The main thing I learned that summer is that I am no salesperson. Of the 200 magazines, I think John sold 190, and I maybe sold 10. We would go to a street; he would take one side, and I took the other. When we reached the end, he would have sold three to four magazines, and I had sold none. To this day, if a child comes to my door, selling something, he or she has a sale. I just can't turn one away, remembering how I felt when I was told "no" again and again.

That year, for the first time, junior camp was held in Palo Duro Canyon, just outside of Amarillo, Texas. We had a wonderful time and enjoyed the crafts and other activities. We traveled with a group from Albuquerque, and we had a good time going and coming as well.

In the summer of 1948, Mother became pregnant with Mary Lou, our youngest sister. She was close to forty years old at this time, and it was a very difficult time for her. She felt terrible and was in bed most of the first trimester. One of the things that really worried her was that she was too sick to make John and me the clothes we needed for the start of school. The other thing that was different was that because she was so sick, she didn't put up the usual argument on us going to church school. She said later that part of the reason she didn't insist, as she did every other year, was that she didn't know how she was going to pay the tuition. She said that it was a lack of faith on her part. She said if she had gone to the church board and explained the circumstances, she felt sure that some of the church members would have helped her with the money until she was able to take care of it herself.

So, John and I attended the local public school that year. I hated it. I wasn't accepted. Because I'm dyslexic, I have always had problems reading aloud, and I just plainly can't spell. We were using the same books that Mother had bought for John, so I was acquainted with them and was really bored in class since I had the books at home. I remember asking the teacher if I brought my own books, would she let me move up into the next class. I'm not sure what she thought, but she didn't let me move up.

On the other hand, John did really well in the public school and never went back to church school. I think it was also about that time that he stopped going to church. He became involved with some of the sports and made some good friends.

After her first trimester, Mother began to feel better, and she said the first thing she did was to make John and me the clothes we needed for school. The whole pregnancy was a difficult one, and from what she said later, she never did feel well the whole time. The doctor she went to was one that Aunt Mary was working for at that time. Our usual family doctor was Dr. Styles, one of the church members, but his real love was being in South America. He said that he felt like he was home when he went down there, and from things I read later, he did a magnificent job with the people there around Lake Titicaca. Unfortunately, he was out of the country during the time that Mother was pregnant with Mary Lou, so he wasn't there to care for her.

Somehow, the doctor that was taking care of Mother didn't realize that because of the way the doctor had delivered Anna, her cervix was so scarred that it couldn't dilate, and he let Mother lay in bed for four days before he took her into the hospital and did a c-section on her. By that time, she was in really bad shape, and Mary Lou was almost dead. Daddy said they had to put a pulmotor on her to get her to breathe. She was smaller than us other children. She weighed four pounds, four ounces at birth, but she did gain well and soon was up to a normal weight for her age. However, Mary Lou was never as healthy as were we other children. More on that later.

Mother was in the hospital for about ten days, and then she went to stay with Aunt Monnie and Uncle Bill until she was stronger. I'm not sure who they got to stay with me and John, but I do remember the first day Mother wasn't there. I got up and started to get ready to go to school, but the girl who was staying with us talked me into staying home with her. I'm sure she didn't have to do too much persuading, either, since I really didn't like going to that school. I'm not sure how Daddy found out that I hadn't been in school, I may have told him, but you can bet that I didn't miss any more days. What really confused me was that the girl who was with us put the blame on me, stating that I had refused to go.

Before Mother came home, Daddy had turned the "bathroom" into a real bathroom. They had finished digging the cesspool. It had to go through the caleche, down to the gravel, which was about ten feet. Before Mother came home, Daddy took John and me into the bathroom and showed us the new toilet and bathtub. He hadn't gotten the water connected to the toilet, but the drainpipe was in place, so it would flush. He showed us how to fill the tank, drawing the water from the tub. He explained that Mother was coming home, but she was unable to lift the bucket of water, so it was going to be our responsibility to be sure the tank was always full.

I was thrilled with my new little sister. By this time, I was eleven years old and was able to be a big help to Mother. Mary Lou was frail and very small, and I was very protective towards her. And in fact, I came to think of her as my baby. She was different from Anna in that she was not comfortable with strangers. She would cry when anyone came near her and would let only the family hold her or play with her. I loved to hold her, give her a bottle, and rock her. I think that's where I learned to sing to the babies, a habit I still have. We developed a very close relationship that lasted until her death in 1963.

It took Mother several months to recover from Mary Lou's birth, but she was soon back to sewing to make money for our schooling. This year, things were different. For one thing, Anna was in school, and we went to different schools. The English and Spanish churches had come together and divided the grades. The first four grades were held in the English church; the upper four grades were at the Spanish church on the corner of Mountain Road and 6th Street. This was in a building behind the church, so it was actually a better arrangement.

My teacher for the first two years was Lucius Martinez, and she was a good teacher. Across from the church was a small park that we used during recess time. We had to cross the street to get to the park, so the city sent out a policeman to set up crossing guards for us. It had a baseball field, a tennis court, and some very nice swings. On the east side of it was a fire station. I wasn't very good at sports, since I was almost blind and couldn't see the ball until it was ready to hit me, so I almost always missed it. Around the park was an adobe fence, plastered with openings, and one of the things we liked to do was walk on the fence. At the corner was one of the openings, and while it was probably the same width as the other openings, because it was cattycornered where the others were straight, it looked wider. We jumped it, and it took a lot of courage to jump that opening.

There were three boys in the school who were crossing guards. My main memory was once when the policeman came to the school to talk to the teacher and the boys. She had been telling us about the problems that had occurred in the school board meeting the night before and was very upset. She was crying, and I remember her saying that she wished the parents got along as well as the students did. Just then, the policeman came. She was embarrassed to let him see her with tears on her face, so she ran behind the piano and talked to him from there. He took the boys outside and gave them a lecture on making their teacher cry, which they were amused to tell us later, since they were not the cause of the problems.

Often, when Miss Martinez would let me, I stayed inside the school room and read. We had a decent library there, and I think I read every book in it. I went to that school from sixth to eighth grade and did well. Of course, I didn't learn to spell, and I continued to have problems reading aloud, but other than that, I managed to keep up with the other children.

> *Mother was always ready to help anyone who needed it.*

Mother was always ready to help anyone who needed it. I remember coming home one day from school and finding a strange man in the kitchen eating. I asked Mother who he was, and after he left, she told me that he had come there, offering to do some work for some food. He was hungry and needed a coat. I don't remember just what had happened to him, but I do remember Mother giving him one of Daddy's coats, which was a fair fit. She wouldn't let him work, but when he left, she handed him a copy of *Steps to Christ* and told him that she wanted him to read that. He assured her that he would, and hopefully, he did.

There was one other incident I remember happening about that time. We still didn't have a car, so we rode the bus to church. As we were leaving church one Sabbath, a visitor stopped Mother and asked her if there was a restaurant close to the church where he and his wife could get something to eat. Mother quickly invited them to our house for the rest of the day. We always had enough food for an extra person or two, and we had a garden with fresh lettuce for a salad. It seemed that he and his wife were in an automobile accident and were stranded in Albuquerque until their car was repaired. They had found the church but had no way of knowing where anything else was in the town. I remember he had a cut over his eye with stiches in it. I was fascinated by the stiches since he didn't have them covered with a dressing. Several months later, on their way back east, they stopped and spent the Sabbath with us again, but this time Mother was prepared, and we rode home in his car.

As I stated earlier, Mary Lou did not like strangers. One Sabbath when we got on the bus to go home, some girls got on who were eating ice cream cones. Mary Lou was about a year old at that time. She was hungry and probably a little tired from being in church. When she saw the girls eating the ice cream, she decided she wanted some, too. Of course, Mother had no way of getting any for her and wouldn't have on the Sabbath anyway. Mary Lou started crying, and the longer she cried, the more upset she became. I tried to get Mother to let me have her, but Mother refused. All the people on the bus were concerned because she was really crying hard. A gentleman came up to Mother and asked if he could take her. Mother tried to explain to him that she didn't readily go to strangers, but he assured her that he was very good with babies, so Mother finally handed Mary Lou to him. When Mary Lou felt his hands on her, she stopped crying, then looked up at him. Her eyes got really big, and then she let out a piercing scream. I was sitting just opposite them, so when she screamed, I stood up and took her. She grabbed me, and when I sat down, she snuggled right into my arms and was asleep in about three minutes.

It was shortly after this that Mother and Daddy decided they needed to buy a car. Since Uncle Anderson had such a good Nash, they decided to get one also. The car they got was a disaster. This was before the day of the automatic transmission, but the stick shift was on the steering wheel column. I can remember Daddy trying to explain to Mother how to use it. Remember, Mother was never a good driver. She didn't enjoy it, and she only did it out of necessity. It had been about ten years since she had driven, except when she went to the drug store to get supplies for Aunt Monnie when we first returned to Albuquerque, so Daddy took her out to teach her how to drive again. Daddy was an excellent driver, and he was a good teacher, but it still took her a while to feel comfortable while driving, and of course, the problems with the Nash didn't help. I can remember her sitting behind the wheel, trying to get the car in gear and hearing it grind. I'm not sure how long they kept that car, but I do know it wasn't long. The next car they got was a little Chevy. That was a good car and served them for several years.

THE 1950s

It was about that time that Mother decided to see if she couldn't start earning more money than she could make with her sewing. Daddy's salary wasn't enough for them to get the things done to the house that needed to be done, and besides, she was finding it increasingly hard to earn enough to cover her expenses with us in church school. Granddad had come to live with us by that time, so there would be someone with us when both she and Daddy were working. She decided she needed to work at night, so she would be with us when we were home, and Granddad and Daddy could take care of Mary Lou while she was sleeping in the daytime.

She had checked into going back to teaching in the public schools, but things had changed since she had married, and she would have had to go to school for at least three semesters to get her bachelor's degree. She asked at several bakeries, since they did most of their baking at night, but since she had no experience and refused to work Friday night, none of them were interested in hiring her. She finally was hired at Saint Joseph Hospital, a Catholic hospital run by the Sisters of Charity, to work in the surgical suite, cleaning the surgical rooms and running the autoclave. If there was an emergency operation, she would also help there by getting any supplies that were needed.

She told of an incident that happened while she was working that year. Early one morning one of the doctors came in and ask Mother if she would help him with a small operation. Of course, she pointed out to him that she wasn't a nurse, but he said that wasn't important, and she knew where the supplies he would need were located. She said yes, and they, together, did the operation, that she later discovered was an abortion. A day or two later the head Mother Superior called Mother aside and questioned her closely about the operation and that was when she discovered it had been an abortion, and since this was a Catholic hospital, the nun was most upset. After questing Mother closely, she decided Mother hadn't knowingly participated in it, so she wasn't reprimanded. However, several days later, the doctor made the remark to Mother, "We really got into trouble, didn't we?"

She enjoyed the work very much and decided she liked medical work, so when they started the training class for the LPNs, Mother joined it. This was the first class in Albuquerque, and I think it was also the first class held in New Mexico. She did well at it and enjoyed learning. She told me about a time when she had to prepare a month's menu as an exercise for her class, which she did as a vegetarian. The teacher was quite skeptical when Mother told her what she was going to do, but after closely examining it, she had to admit that a person could get all the vitamins and minerals needed, along with sufficient protein, in that diet. The course was for one year, and she graduated as an LPN. I don't think she had to take state boards though.

Rebecca (in third row, second from left) with her graduating class in 1951.

Their uniforms were yellow, and they had a yellow cap that they wore while in training. It was emphasized that they were NOT to wear the cap any place but in the hospital. One of the girls had taken her cap with her to watch a baseball game and put it on to show the people with her what it looked like. The TV camera swung around just then, so she was seen in every home in Albuquerque that was watching the game. Of course, some of the people from the hospital saw it. Daddy saw it, so he later asked Mother about it, and she told him that she, the girl, was given a severe lecture Monday.

The hospital hired Mother after she graduated, but again, she was working nights, and she didn't do well with night work. She was definitely a lark, so she went to Bataan Hospital and started working there. She was there for just a little over a year but quit because she felt they didn't accept her training as an LPN. She worked at the osteopathic hospital for about a year, I think, then Saint Joseph called her and asked her to come back there and take a position training the aides. She agreed, and she was there until about 1954, when she went to work at Kirkland Airforce Base. She was able to earn more money there, and the work wasn't as hard physically.

It was while she was working at St. Joe's that Mary Lou had her first attack of rheumatic fever. By that time, I was boarding at Sandia View Academy and was home by 1:30 p.m. each day. Anna was home from school by 3:30 p.m., and Mary Lou, who was five years old, was still at home. Mother asked me to bring Anna and Mary Lou to town to meet her when she got off work at 5:30 p.m., as she wanted to do some shopping. We had been to two stores, I think, when Mary Lou started crying, saying that her legs hurt. Mother looked at her legs, and her knees were swollen. She left Mary Lou there, sitting on a bench with Anna, while she and I hurriedly finished what shopping was necessary. We caught the bus to go home, but when we got off the bus, we still had five blocks to walk, and Mary Lou just couldn't walk. By that time, we had a phone, so Mother called home and asked John and our cousin, Larry, who happened to be there that evening, to come to help us. I remember John, putting Mary Lou on his shoulders, and Larry taking the floor lamp that Mother had bought, and thus, we proceeded home. The next day, Mother took Mary Lou to see Dr. Styles, and he pronounced that she needed to stay in bed until the rheumatic fever had run its course. She was put on penicillin and aspirin. It was over a month that she was pretty much bedfast but was restricted in her activities for almost a year. I was with her one time when she was taken to Dr. Styles' office for lab work. She didn't whimper when they drew the blood, but she did look at me and said, very quietly, "That hurts."

Dr. Styles told Mother that it would be a good idea to remove Mary Lou's tonsils, as this possibly was part of the reason for her having rheumatic fever. Daddy agreed, but Granddad was violently opposed to it. When they decided to have them removed, Granddad moved out to stay with Uncle Bill and Aunt Monnie, and he refused to even see her afterward for several months. This was very confusing to Mary Lou, as he was her main caregiver. Eventually he did move back in, but during the time when she really needed him, he wasn't there for her. She didn't have any heart involvement from that attack, but she had another attack two years later, and she did experience damage to her heart. From that time on, she was never strong.

After Granddad came to live with us, it was decided to build an addition to the east side of the house. Since the new addition would cover part of the cesspool, it meant that they had to bridge over it, and Daddy did that by laying a good, firm, concrete foundation. At the same time, they also dug a basement under the house. The opening to it was in the middle of the screened-in porch. The southeast part of the new addition was the kitchen, then the porch, where they placed the washing machine, and the northeast corner was turned into a room for Granddad. Its only opening was onto the porch, so it was more private for him. What had been the kitchen was made into a dining room.

The author with her siblings in 1952.

It was about that time that Daddy was able to find the dining table we used from then on. It was solid oak, with four leaves to put in it, which made it double in size. When it was without the leaves, it could comfortably seat two people on each side; when completely open, it was easily able to accommodate five people on the long sides. From then on, when we had a family get-together, it was always held at our house. When Daddy first got the table, it was in bad repair. It had been stored in a basement for many years, so he had to completely refinish it, but when he was finished, it was a beautiful piece of furniture. One of my memories was Daddy putting a two by twelve board on the backside of the table as seating for all the children. Incidentally, when they moved to Weatherford, that table went to Anna, who still has it to this day.

I think it was about that time when they retired the old stove and got Mother a new one. It was much nicer and larger than the first one she had. The oven was what she especially appreciated; it was much roomier than the one in the little stove. We also had a Servel refrigerator, which used natural gas. I have the impression that it was Granddad who bought it, and he also got one for Uncle Bill and Aunt Monnie. I don't remember what we used before that; it must have been an ice box.

It was while Granddad was staying with Uncle Bill and Aunt Monnie that he fell and broke his hip. For many years, he had belonged to the Moose Lodge, mainly because he planned on retiring there when he became unable to work, or as he said, when "he became useless." After he was released from the hospital, he came back to our house. He applied to the Moose Lodge to be accepted into Moose Haven, their home for retired members and was informed that they only took people who were mobile. To put it mildly, he was upset. He had belonged to the Moose Lodge for many years and had really counted on living out his final years there. He never paid another penny to them, and I never heard him speak of them again.

For some reason, he got the idea that even though the doctor had put a plate in his femur, he needed a year to recover. He stayed in a wheelchair for one solid year. At the end of the year, he was very weak and unable to walk any distance. He moved to Ft. Sumner to stay with his sister, Rebecca, who lived on her ranch. He said later that he was determined to walk again, so he started out, trying to rebuild his strength. In the year, his leg had shortened about two inches, so one of the first things he had to have done was to get his shoe built up that length. He also used crutches, more for balance than anything else. He sometimes used a walker but preferred the crutches. It took him almost a week to be able to walk to the front door, then a day or two to walk across the porch. Within another week, he was walking across the yard, then he started down the road, going one fence post farther each day. He stayed with her for almost a year, and when he came back to our house, he had them measure how far he was walking each day. It was just over two and a half miles out, one fence post at a time.

One other thing he developed as the result of his surgery was what the doctor called a "sterile abscess" in the incision site. It drained for the rest of his life. At first it required a large bandage, but with time, it decreased to a small enough amount that a large piece of tape covered it and only needed to be changed daily.

By the time Granddad moved back in with Daddy and Mother, I was attending Sandia View Academy (SVA) and was only home during the holidays and vacation time in the summer. Mother, by this time, was back at St. Joe's and in charge of training the nurses' aides. I worked at St. Joe's each summer to earn the money for my clothing and other things that I needed, which was a real help to Mother.

It was about this time that John, my brother, joined the Marine Corps. He was sent to New Delhi after he finished basic training as a guard for the embassy there. This led to his future employment as a worker in the Diplomatic Corp, staffing the consulates and embassies until he retired. He met his first wife there; she was a secretary in the embassy. Her name was Betty Coyle, and she also enjoyed that kind of work, so she was happy when John was hired by the Diplomatic Corp. They served in the Azores Islands then Japan. They were sent to Chad, and while there, she was given an antibiotic that destroyed the platelets in her blood, causing her death in 1969.

> It was also about this time that the church in Albuquerque started its first Pathfinder Club. In order to work in it, Mother had to earn her Master Guide accreditation.

It was also about this time that the church in Albuquerque started its first Pathfinder Club. In order to work in it, Mother had to earn her Master Guide accreditation. She had no problem with anything except earning some of the honors, and she had to take a test on Bible doctrines and church history. She said later that she really dreaded taking the test on Bible doctrines. She had heard it was very tough, but since she had been studying her

Sabbath School lessons every day, she had no problems; however, when it came to the church history, she almost failed. She had gotten most of her church history from reading the Spirit of Prophecy and Sister White. Other than mentioning the fatal flaw in 1888 and the alpha of apostasy in 1905, the books didn't go into a lot of the real problems besetting the church and certainly didn't do any character assassination. Therefore, she still thought of the church as relatively pure. This aroused her curiosity, so she began to do some studying on church history and became well-acquainted with some of the problems that were, and are, being brought into the church.

She mentioned the time she and Anna worked on their hiking honor. It required three five-mile hikes in one week, two ten-mile hikes in a month, and one fifteen-mile hike. Mother was always a great walker, so it wasn't hard for her to do all the hikes, but the fifteen-mile hike was hard on some of the younger members, including Anna. They started out, spent the night in tents, and ended up at the Jenkins' home. The Jenkins were members of the church, and their son, Westley, was among the hikers. A truck carried their tents and other equipment, and when it passed them on the way to Jenkins' home, some of the hikers got on it and rode instead of walking the rest of the way. Anna was among that group. She still had several miles to walk, but after they left there, she decided to get out of the car and walk the needed miles home, which she did, so she earned her honor.

I also remember her talking about when the Pathfinder Club had first started, John had come home on furlough. She talked him into giving the kids lessons on marching. Since he had just come out of basic training, he was very good at it, and they really learned how to do all the commands that are commonly used in the military. Of course, from then on, one of the older boys could teach the younger ones, so it worked out well.

During her active years, Mother started or helped start two Pathfinder Clubs: the one in Albuquerque and the one in Weatherford, Texas. She never lost her love for teaching children and was always active with the children as long as she was able. Since Mary Lou was a member of the Pathfinder Club in Albuquerque, Mother participated in it. On one of

> *During her active years, Mother started or helped start two Pathfinder Clubs: the one in Albuquerque and the one in Weatherford, Texas. She never lost her love for teaching children and was always active with the children as long as she was able.*

their camporees, they took a group of kids down to the mountains near Cloudcroft. In telling me about it, Mother said that just before that, she had done something really stupid, she didn't remember what, but she was afraid to ask Daddy if she could have the car for the weekend. It would mean that he had to stay at the Veteran's Hospital while they were gone, but he usually didn't object when she wanted to use the car for an event that included Mary Lou. However, this time, she didn't want to ask him, so she told Mary Lou if she could get permission from Daddy, they would go. Mary Lou asked Daddy, and, as usual, he didn't object, so they went. The place they camped was in the mountains, and it was cold in the mornings, so she was wearing her coat with an apron over it. She had taken a couple of days off from work, and from what they both said, it was a very enjoyable camping time for all the group. Mother said that she came back with her nose sunburned despite the cold.

> One other thing that really impressed me was the way she handled her money. She paid tithe on what she earned each pay period, not her take-home pay.

One other thing that really impressed me was the way she handled her money. She paid tithe on what she earned each pay period, not her take-home pay. She and Daddy always filed a joint income tax return, so what they got back was already tithed. Daddy, as I said, was raised in the Primitive Baptist Church, who don't pay their ministers, so he couldn't understand our church's stand on tithing. He was always complaining that Mother supported the church by herself, since she always gave an offering, besides tithing. As I mentioned before, he couldn't understand the reason she wanted us to go to and pay for church school when there was a good public school close by. By her paying tithe on her actual earnings, she decreased the contention between them.

At St. Joe's, the director of nurses had changed, and the new director decided she wanted to be in charge of training the nurses' aides herself, so Mother was put back on floor duty. That wouldn't have upset her, but she was required to work nights and that did. As I said, she didn't work well at night, so she started looking for another job. She took the test for government employment and was hired to work at Kirkland Air Force Base as a file clerk, with quite an increase in pay. Since I was in the academy and the two younger girls were in church school, the additional money was greatly appreciated.

She said the job was very boring. It consisted of filing IBM cards and checking that they were made out correctly. They covered everything from nuts and bolts that cost a few cents to very expensive jet engines and such that cost thousands of dollars.

Since she did very little walking in her job, she started walking to work every morning. The base was located about four miles from our house. She left about an hour early and walked until someone offered her a ride, which was usually about twenty minutes before she needed to be at work. She made some good friends by accepting rides over the years. She stayed with that job until she retired after ten years there. I'm not sure how she got home in the evening since Daddy was working at the Veterans Hospital from 4:00 p.m. to midnight, and he took the car. The bus service wasn't set up to be helpful in this situation, since a person would have to get on the bus, go downtown, and transfer to another bus, altogether taking about two hours. It may be that she had a regular ride with one of the other people there who were going that way. While she was walking, she observed the flora alongside the road. She found it very interesting that there were many kinds of wild grass, even in that arid climate. She said she had identified about twenty if I remember correctly. The first part of the way was settled, with houses or businesses, but after she crossed Gibson Street, there were no houses. It was all government land. It was there that she saw different kinds of grass.

Usually she had no trouble, but one morning as she was walking, two young dogs joined her. They were boxer puppies, full grown but still puppies. As usual, the wind was blowing, and since it was cold weather, she was wearing a long coat. The wind was flapping the edges of her coat, and the dogs started grabbing at them. She tried to drive them away, but they didn't stop. They were getting rather fierce, tearing her coat, and biting her legs. Although Mother was never a hysterical person, she did become hysterical over this. She ran up to one of the houses and began frantically beating on the door. The lady opened the door, saw the situation, pulled Mother inside, and let her regain her composure. In fact, I think she took Mother home in her car. She explained that the dogs were owned by the family down the street and were usually confined to the backyard, but they had somehow gotten out. They weren't vicious, just playful, but that didn't undo the damage they had done to Mother's coat or her legs.

There were regular people who were hired to work there, but there were also some of the military personal in the office. They were usually only there for a short time, maybe a year or two. They also were in and out, so the regular people did the largest amount of the work. Over the years, she met many young men through this, and I'm sure made a deep impression on many of them. Usually, during the lunch break, she would sit at her desk and eat her sandwich and read her Bible. Most of them highly respected her, and if there was a Bible question asked, she was the final word on it. Their language was also carefully monitored while they were in her presence. Her boss, Mary Kay, told Mother once that she really appreciated it because before Mother had come, the language in the office could get really raunchy.

As I had mentioned earlier, Mother wasn't raised in a family where there was much teasing or joking, but she could, upon occasion, pull off a good joke. This happened while working at Kirkland Base. As usual, the room where she worked drew names for their Christmas party. One of the young airmen repeatedly stated that while he would draw a name, he really didn't want anything given to him. Mother went to Mary Kay, who was the supervisor, and told her that she, Mother, wanted his name. Mary Kay gave it to her. Her plan was to give him an empty box with a false bottom in it and put a ten dollar bill under the false bottom. When she told Daddy about that, he suggested that he have one of the patients at the VA hospital, who did leatherwork, make him a nice wallet, so that is what she did.

When the gifts were handed out, the young airman opened his present, which was, to all appearances, an empty box. When he protested, Mother said to him, "Well, that's what you wanted!" However, he, knowing Mother fairly well, gave the box a good looking over and spied the false bottom. He was very pleased with the very nice, tooled leather wallet. The main difference in the teasing that Mother and Daddy did was that Mother was very careful to never hurt anyone with her teasing or jokes. Daddy really didn't see anything wrong in hurting another, either their feelings or physically. If he got a laugh out of it, he enjoyed the joke.

It was while she was working there that for some reason, during a cut back in military financing, the base cut their staff, and Mother was one who was laid off. It was understood that when the funds were available, she and the others would be called back to work, but in the meanwhile, they were laid off. They could and did draw unemployment. Mother told me that it was about five months, and that was one of the best vacations she ever had, paid for sitting at home. When President Kennedy took office, one of the first things he did was increase the military budget, so Mother and the others were recalled.

It may have been during the time that she was off work that she and the two girls drove to Texas. Daddy had gone earlier, and for some reason, he needed Mother to come and get him. He must have gone down via Greyhound bus, since she had the car. They left immediately after church on Sabbath and drove almost as far as the state line between Texas and New Mexico. When they got there, it was dark, so she drove off the main highway for about a mile, then turned into an open field until they were out of sight of the road. Since they were in a station wagon, they slept in the back. The next morning, they started driving again. When they got to Clovis, she looked at the gas tank, but it was only about one-fourth down, so she didn't stop to fill up.

What she didn't realize was that Texas, at that time, enforced the Blue Law, and all the gas stations were closed on Sunday. When the gage indicated they had about one-fourth tank left, she started looking for somewhere to get gas, but she couldn't find a station that was open. By that time, she was really worried, but, as she said, she had heard that after the tank registered empty, there was still some gas in it. So, holding her breath, as she put it, she continued on, and she actually did reach Aunt Ruby's house. The next morning Daddy took the car to the closest gas station and put in twenty-one and a half gallons. (Daddy always thought it had a twenty-gallon tank.)

One other incident that happened was quite amusing to Mother. As I said, she wasn't a very good driver and would often get into some kind of trouble that needed someone to extract her out of. They had planted a row of sapling silver leaf maples close to where they parked the car at the house. Somehow, in trying to back up, she got one of the trees caught between the front of the car and the bumper. (In those days the bumpers weren't molded to the car as they are now.) John was home, so she went inside and asked him to untangle the car for her. He went outside, looked at it, then came back inside and asked, "How on earth did you manage to do that?" Since it was a flexible sapling, she had obviously caught it with the bumper, then as she pulled forward, it had snapped back into place. Somehow, he managed to untangle the car, and she was able to go where she had intended to go.

Not too long after going to work at Kirkland, Mother bought the piano. Anna was about ten years old, and Mother wanted to have her start taking lessons. She had wanted to give me piano lessons when I was younger, but they just didn't have the money, so it wasn't meant to be. I well remember when Mother took me to the store and had me pick out the piano. I played a few chords and chose the one that had the tone I liked best. We were choosing among several that were used, but that didn't matter. It was a good piano and served us well. I remember the salesman telling us that he would try to find a piano bench to go with it, and he did. Anna's first teacher was Pastor Schram's wife. She was a very good teacher, and Anna did well under her. Before long, she was the pianist for the junior department, which was very good training. She was able to take music lessons until she graduated from college and is a fine musician today.

At Christmas time in 1955, I went with a group from SVA to Sante Fe to help with Harvest Ingathering—an effort to solicit funds for missions and local relief work—and I met Jim Russ there. We were married on January 30, 1956, so I dropped out of school and moved to Sante Fe with him. Therefore, I lacked one semester before graduating.

It was sometime during the years when I was gone that the two churches decided to build a school building. If I remember right, they borrowed the money from the conference, and the church people pledged the money to repay the loan. Mother was made treasurer of it, and I remember her talking about it. She showed me the system she had, where she entered the money that was paid and who had donated it every week. She showed me that it was the people who had pledged $10 or $15 dollars weekly or semiweekly who paid it off, not the ones who made a big contribution and then paid nothing more.

THE 1960s

In the fall of 1956, Jim and I moved to the Los Angeles area. There he started working for RCA, and learned how to repair color televisions that were just coming out then. Our three daughters were born there: Marie on February 14, 1957; Michele on May 6, 1958; and Renee on January 28, 1960. Jim was killed in April, 1960, so I moved back to Albuquerque in July of that year.

It was shortly after I moved back from California when we received word that John was going to marry Betty Coyle, one of the secretaries in the embassy at New Delhi, India. Their honeymoon was their trip home. Betty was a pretty woman, very refined and loved that kind of life. They moved back to Albuquerque but didn't stay long. John went to work for the National Cash Register Company, with whom he had worked before his service, but he wasn't happy with his job, as it consisted of him being out of town several days at a time most weeks. As a new groom, that wasn't to his or Betty's liking, so he applied to join the Diplomatic Corps, as a staff in the embassies and consulates in the different countries.

When he was hired, they moved back to Washington, DC, for training, which was more to Betty's liking, as her family lived there. By that time, she was pregnant with Ken, their first child. I remember Mother talking about the baby shower she gave for them. Since they were moving soon, everyone gave them money. Mother made up a little packet of paper diapers and put money with it. Others obtained or drew pictures of the things they would have bought and gave the money for that. It worked out very well. So, Ken was born in Virginia, and they were transferred to the Azores Islands when he was just a few weeks old.

Mother was church clerk during those years also, so she was on the church board. By this time, Elder Schram had been called to the conference office, and if I'm not mistaken, the next pastor was H. M. S. Richards Jr. I went to church regularly when I moved back in with Mother and Daddy, a widow with three small children. I got a job working at Bataan Hospital, which was just down the road from the Veteran's Hospital, where Daddy worked. I went to work at 3:00 p.m., and he went to work at 4:00 p.m., but since he always went early to take a shower and dress, it worked out well for me. I would then wait in the downstairs waiting room for him to pick me up after he was off work. It must have been very trying for Mother to have four generations in her home, but she never complained. After I started receiving Social Security for the children, I rented a small house and moved out, with her encouragement.

One of their neighbors was a woman named Sally Meyers, who had three small children about the same age as mine, so we became good friends, much to Mother's disappointment. She wasn't a Christian, and I only too willingly followed her. It was through her that I met my second husband, a solder at Sandia Base, who was there for training, on temporary duty from El Paso. I moved to El Paso to be near him until we were married.

Daddy and Sally were good friends and spent quite a bit of time together. Shortly before this, Daddy had driven to Ft. Sumner to visit Aunt Rebecca. She had needed some help, and Daddy was always willing to help in any way he could. It was about a four-hour drive from Albuquerque to Ft. Sumner, and when he arrived there, before driving on to her ranch, he stopped at a bar to go to the bathroom. He maybe had drunk a beer while there, but he certainly wasn't drunk; however, when he got into the car and started driving, a policeman, who had probably seen him exit the bar, pulled him over and gave him a ticket for DWI. In talking with the people there, he was advised to plead guilty, as he had a clean driving record, and this was his first offense. He did, and his driver's license was suspended for one year, plus he had to pay a big fine. Mother had to go down and get him, since he couldn't drive. During that year, Sally did a lot of driving for him, and he really appreciated it.

One big problem with Sally was the lack of discipline of her children. I was with her once when we entered a store. She told her children that she didn't want to see them until she was ready to leave, and apparently, she did this most times when she entered a store. She explained, "They are big enough to look out for themselves," meaning the store. She soon had quite a reputation among the stores, and Daddy was in a store with her once when the manager brought one of her children to her and told her to leave and not to return. Daddy was horrified and refused to let her take him to any store from then on, but she would still take him places, if he needed to go.

Another habit she had was to tell her children that she didn't want to see them until mealtime when they went outside to play. Until then, Mother and Daddy had never locked their house, but they started to do so when Mother came home one evening and found a bucket of dirt dumped on her bed. As I said, Daddy enjoyed working with wood and had quite a collection of tools needed for some of the finer work. The children got into his workshop and damaged some of the tools, so he started locking that up also. Fortunately, he turned the electricity off at the main when he left, so they couldn't run any of the big tools.

When Mary Lou was about ten, Mother started her studying music on the accordion. She also did well. There was a school not too far from the house, and Mary Lou went there weekly. She started out renting a fairly small accordion, then when she became more proficient, Mother got her a really nice accordion. Mother didn't have the money to pay cash for it, so she financed it. I was there when the payment booklet came in the mail. Daddy opened the envelope, saw that it was a payment, and blew up. He called the company and told them that he hadn't borrowed any money from them and didn't appreciate them trying to gouge money out of him.

The person who was listening to him very calmly let him finish, then said, "Mr. Ivie, this is the payment for your daughter's new accordion."

He apologized, turned to me with a sheepish look, and said, "I guess I should have talked to Mother before I called them."

One interesting side note was that in December that year, Anna, Stanley, the boy she later married, and I went out as a team to Harvest Ingathering. Anna played the accordion while she and I sang, and Stanley went to the door and did the soliciting. As I remember, we raised quite a bit of money that year doing that.

In late 1961 or early 1962, Grandmother started having small strokes, then she had a major one. She wasn't paralyzed, but she was no longer able to live alone. Her doctor wanted her placed in a "good nursing home," and he recommended one in Las Vegas, New Mexico. She was sent there and loved it. The attendants were good to her, and she had people from one of the local churches visiting her frequently. Mother and I went up to see her every month, and she enjoyed that, too. The last weekend of May, Mother, Mary Lou, my girls, and I drove up to see her. She was in bed. She said she didn't feel good but was happy to see us. Mary Lou took the girls outside to play, while Mother and I talked with Grandmother. We talked for a while, then she dozed off to sleep. We waited for another thirty minutes or so, and when she didn't wake up, we left. We didn't know that she was having another stroke, and she died that evening. Mother wrote to John to inform him and started her letter by saying, "I didn't realize until I wrote the date that today is my birthday." She told John not to try to come home. It was just too far, and her death wasn't too surprising. I know she missed Grandmother, but it wasn't a real tragedy.

In 1963, Mary Lou started attending Sandia View Academy. There were three students going. All three were freshmen and were driven by Pastor Fiedler, since his daughter, Diana, was one of them. The other two were Arthur Layba and Mary Lou. Mother drove her to the pastor's house every morning, then went home and left for work. Anna was at Keene, Texas, attending SWJC, and I was living in El Paso. John was working in the Azores, so Mary Lou was the only child left at home.

I think it was the morning of December 16. Mother drove Mary Lou to Pastor Fiedler's home, then went home, and went to work. Sometime later, I think about 9:00 a.m., one of the service men came over to Mother and said, "Mrs. Ivie, I just heard on the radio that there was an auto accident, and your daughter was killed."

Mother grabbed the phone and started trying to call home, but all she got was a busy signal. Meanwhile, her boss, Mary Kay, called the police, then turned to Mother, and said, "I'm afraid it's true." She then told one of the other women who worked there to take Mother home and to stay with her as long as Mother needed her. As they drove up to the house, a police car drove up and stopped. Mother, of course, went inside. The other woman talked to the policeman, and he told her that he had come to notify the family, since each time they called, they also received a busy signal. She told him that Mother knew, and she was going to take them to the hospital, where Mary Lou's body was. Mother went inside and told Daddy that there had been an accident, and they were needed at the hospital, so they left with the other woman driving them. I think it was Uncle Bill who took them home from the hospital.

We were told later that the accident was caused by a driver cutting back too soon after passing. Elder Fiedler cut his wheels to the right, hit a soft shoulder, and the car rolled three and a half times, ending up in the median strip of Interstate 125. The driver's door opened, and he went out on the second roll. Mary Lou went out on the third. (This was before seat belts.) They were both killed. The car rested upside down, with both doors open, and Arthur lying partly inside with a cut eleven inches long on the top of his head. The first car that stopped was a doctor and his office nurse going to Albuquerque from Santa Fe. He put a pressure bandage on Arthur's head, put him in the back of his car, and took him to Presbyterian Hospital. The nurse in charge of the emergency room was the wife of the Bible teacher at Sandia View, so she knew Arthur, signed the permit, and sent him immediately to surgery. The best neurosurgeon in Albuquerque was in the hospital, and before Arthur's parents were able to get there, he was in the operating room. Shortly later, the ambulance came in with the bodies of Pastor Fiedler and Mary Lou. She looked at them and then asked, "Where's Diana?" The ambulance people hadn't seen her, so a search was started for her. She was found over a mile away, wandering, completely in a daze, and unhurt.

Of course, the school was immediately notified, as was the conference and the other two families. I'm not sure who called SWJC, but Anna was notified and was on her way to Ft. Worth before Mother and Daddy were notified. The phone line was busy because Granddad had used the phone the night before and hadn't put it back on the cradle correctly. Mother said later that she thought it was a blessing because this way she was able to be with Daddy when he was told.

I didn't have a phone, so I received a note from a taxi driver, asking me to call a certain telephone operator. When I did, she connected me to Mother, and she told me of the accident. I told her I would be there as soon as I could get there. She told me not to try to drive but to fly up, so I did. When I got off the plane, I saw the headlines on the newspaper: EIGHT KILLED ON NEW MEXICO HIGHWAYS TODAY. Of course, their names were listed, so everyone in town knew about it. James McCraw, my first husband's uncle, was a high official in the Atomic Energy Commission. He called Mother and asked if he could do anything to help. She hadn't been able to notify John, even though she had tried the phone numbers he had given her. James' reply was, "Don't worry, I'll see that it's done," and he did. John called later that evening. He had been told of Mary Lou's death but not the details. He offered to try to fly home, but Mother told him that it wasn't necessary. It was just too far, and he probably couldn't get there in time for the funeral anyway.

When I walked into the house, it was full of people, standing room only. I don't remember how late they stayed, but the next few days were very busy. Both Mother and Daddy were completely devastated, so most of the arranging fell on me. I had never done anything like that before and was completely in over my head, but we did manage to muddle through. I remember the funeral director calling me to ask who we wanted for pallbearers. Someone was there, I don't remember who, and suggested we have the boys from SVA do that, so I called the school, and they arranged that.

Daddy called his brother, Hubert, and Audie, his wife, and their sister, Ruby, and her husband, Andrew, who lived in Texas, and they all came. This was less than a month after President Kennedy was killed in Dallas, and feelings were still running high. After they got into New Mexico, a car tried to run them off the road, and one of the people yelled at them, "Go home! We don't want any president killers here." Poor Aunt Ruby was really upset by this. In telling us about it, she was crying and said, "I didn't have anything to do with President Kennedy's death."

I think it was when Daddy called Aunt Ruby to tell her of Mary Lou's death that he told her he wanted a certain song sung at Mary Lou's funeral, but he couldn't remember it, only a few words. He had mentioned it to Mother, but it was one she had never heard of before, so she wasn't any help to him. He sang the few words to Aunt Ruby, and she recognized them, but couldn't remember the song, either. She called a friend, and together they were able to bring the song to mind. None of us had ever heard it, and no one at the church had ever heard it, but one of the ladies managed to find a copy, and it was sung. It was "The Wayfaring Stranger." It is a beautiful song, and one I will always associate with that funeral.

Mother and Daddy picked out the casket, and we took her clothes down the next day. Before her body was shown, we, as a family, went in to see it. Her normal complexion was somewhat dark, reflecting the Native American blood in us. They had her made up with a peaches and cream complexion. Daddy took one look at her and started screaming, "That's not my baby! That's not my baby!" Of course, the funeral director came immediately. Mother got Daddy out of room, and I took out a recent colored picture of Mary Lou and gave it to them. They put some suntan powder on her, which made her look much more natural. While I was there, I did some other work on her. She obviously had landed on her head; her forehead was badly bruised, and they had covered it with thick pancake makeup that had obscured her eyebrow. I took a pencil and drew in her eyebrow, recombed her hair, fixed her dress more as she wore it, then we brought Daddy back in. That time he was satisfied that it looked like her.

I will add one other thing here, Granddad refused to attend Mary Lou's funeral. He said he wanted to remember her as she was. It would have been a big support to Mother, I think, but he was adamant about it. All the rest of the family was there. Aunt Mary, Uncle Bill, and Aunt Monnie attended the same church, and they supplied the food for the meal after the funeral. I think most of the members of their church attended as well. And of course, all the people from Sandia View and our church were there.

Her funeral was very large. The room where it was held wasn't large enough to hold all the people. They had chairs all down the hall. The mortuary is located on a hill, and the cemetery is under the hill, in plain sight from it. By the road, it's about a mile, but as the crow flies, maybe a third of a mile. When we pulled up to the grave site, the cars were still leaving the mortuary.

The other thing I remember was the quantity of food that was brought to the house. Of course, none of us were thinking about cooking, and it wasn't necessary. Anytime anyone got hungry, all they had to do was go to the kitchen and get something, and there was a large selection. Mother said that after everyone left, she put the extra food in the freezer, and they ate from it for several months. Another thing I remember was the kindness of one of the church members, Sister Swingle, who came and stayed at the house while we were attending to all the details. She was the mother of Stanley, the boy that Anna later married.

Mary Lou's funeral was held on Thursday, and Elder Fiedler's was on Friday. His was held at the church, and the church was full. Of course, the people from the conference were there, and they conducted the funeral. We didn't go the graveside service; they took me to the airport, and I flew home. I don't know how long Anna stayed, probably until after the new year, as it was so close to Christmas, and that was good for Mother and Daddy. At least they had someone there for a few weeks to help them.

I went back up in February to help Mother clean out Mary Lou's room. She had just closed the door and not gone into it until I arrived. I was shocked at the change in both Mother and Daddy. Mother had lines in her face that hadn't been there before, but Daddy's was really ravaged. His hair, which had been black, with just a few gray hairs at his temples, was now completely gray.

The way they grieved was also quite noticeable. Mother was saddened. She missed Mary Lou, but she had "the blessed hope." Mother knew that Mary Lou had given her heart to the Lord, and she had been baptized when she was about ten, I think, but she really knew and loved the Lord. There was no doubt in Mother's mind that when our Lord returns, she will be among those who will be raised up to meet Him.

Daddy had nothing. I heard him say several times, "I hadn't seen her for almost a week before she was killed." He determined at that time to change, so he could be in heaven with her. Before the accident, he had been drinking heavily. He got off work at midnight, and often went to a bar and stayed there until it closed at 2:00 a.m. On his days off, he spent most of his time at a bar. In fact, it had gotten so bad that Mother was thinking of leaving him. As she told me once, with the money that she was making at Kirkland, she could support the girls and herself. However, from the time that he learned of her death until just before his own death in 1985, he never had another drink.

I stayed for about a week then returned home. I remember taking a lot of things I really didn't want, but Mother wanted them out of the house, so I took them. I think it was good for Mother to have my girls around at that time. It helped her, and I know it helped Daddy. He was always partial to my youngest daughter, Renee, and she helped divert him for the time we were there.

The nurses who worked with Daddy noticed the change in him, the hopelessness in his face, so one of them, being a Christian, invited him to go to church with her. He went two or three times, but he wasn't happy there and expressed his dissatisfaction to Mother. Her reply was "You were raised in the Primitive Baptist Church, so why not go there?" He did and was much more satisfied. Mother always went with him, and they attended regularly. You'll remember that Daddy often complained about the money Mother gave to the church. She continued to return tithe and offerings, but it always vexed him. However, after attending his church and hearing one of the elders in the church make a plea for some money to meet one of the pressing needs of the church, he turned to Mother and asked what she thought of them giving an offering. She told him that it was very much all right, that it was a gift to God, so he happily wrote out a check.

Mary Lou's funeral cost was covered by the car insurance, so the money they collected from her life insurance was an additional bonus. The school also had an insurance policy on the children that covered them from the time they left home until they returned home, and that paid off as well. Altogether, it amounted to several thousand dollars.

Before Mary Lou's death, she and Mother had spent the Sabbaths together, but after her death, Mother had to keep the Sabbath afternoons alone. Daddy almost always had a ball game of some kind blaring on the TV until it was time for him to go to work, so her method of finding some quiet and peace was to go to their room, close the door, and read one of the church papers. This annoyed Daddy, as he would have liked her to join him in watching the games, but she wouldn't for two reasons. One, it was the Sabbath, and the other being that she never cared to watch games on TV. She would sit with him on Sundays, but since his interest was on the game, there was very little conversation between them until a commercial came on. He watched a lot of TV, which was something that never interested Mother. She did have her favorite shows. They usually watched *The Price is Right* and *Let's Make a Deal* together, but she wasn't interested in anything much more than the news. I remember her telling me that after Daddy died, she had much more time to think of spiritual things since her attention wasn't distracted by the noise of the TV. As she put it, "I listened to a lot of TV."

Daddy was determined to move back to Texas. He had two brothers and a sister who lived west of Ft. Worth, so he decided to settle in that area. With the money from Mary Lou's insurance, he purchased about three acres of land just east of Weatherford, behind where his brother Hubert lived. The original owner at one time owned a large ranch, but his wife was dying of cancer, and he sold most of it to pay for her treatment. Mother and Daddy didn't have enough money to build a house on it, but, with their savings, they managed to build a large metal building, have a well dug, and put in a septic system. There were neighbors, so electricity was no problem, and natural gas was also available. Daddy, who had lived in that area as a young person, insisted on digging a storm cellar. Mother said later that if she had known how afraid he was of tornadoes, she would never have consented to moving back to Texas.

Shortly after they bought the land, they were in a fairly severe auto accident themselves. Uncle Hubert was driving and hit another car. He wasn't given a ticket, but Daddy always blamed him for it, and it probably wouldn't have happened if Daddy had been driving. None of them were seriously hurt, but Daddy had a bad cut on his forehead, and as always happens with a scalp wound, it bled freely. He was taken to the local hospital, and it was stitched, but he was anemic from the loss of blood. He didn't recover, and even though he tried to return to work, he just didn't have the strength to do the work, so he was retired with 100 percent disability.

Mother wanted to complete her, as she put it, forty quarters, so she continued to work for about another two years, if I'm not mistaken. That left Daddy free to go back and forth to Weatherford, which he did. He planted fruit trees and had the building erected, dug the storm cellar, and got things ready for their move. They knew they would get enough money from selling the property in Albuquerque to build a house on their land, so he installed sheetrock on the inside of the metal building and prepared it as a place for them to live in until the house was sold. They lived in one half; the other half was used as his shop, where he had all his tools for cabinetmaking.

About the time Mother retired, they arranged for Aunt Mary, who had never married, and Granddad to live in their house, rent free. It would be a help to both of them and wouldn't leave the house empty. They left them there, thinking it would be good for them while they made one of their trips to Weatherford. When they returned, Aunt Mary was vehement. She said she wouldn't live "with that old devil," and she promptly went down and filed a lawsuit against Mother and Daddy, among other things, charging them with bilking Grandad of all his savings. Daddy was furious; Mother was devastated. That her own sister could do that to them was beyond her comprehension. It delayed their moving for over a year. Finally, partly I think through the intersession of Uncle Bill, the lawsuit was dropped, but Daddy never forgave Aunt Mary. Meanwhile, Granddad moved into a small house on the north side of Albuquerque.

John had, meanwhile, served his term in the Azores. He had returned to the Washington, DC, area for further training and then was sent to Japan. Their family was increased by a daughter, Margaret, and on the way, John spent some time with Mother and Daddy. He had Ken, his son, with him. Betty had remained in Arlington, Virginia, for some medical treatment and flew directly to the west coast with Margaret, so they didn't have the privilege of seeing them, but they did enjoy their time with John and their grandson. Daddy always loved being around babies and this was a very special time for him.

Anna finished school at SWJC and moved to Lincoln, Nebraska, to earn her bachelor's. I, meanwhile, had moved to Kansas to be with my husband, so we were well scattered. While living in El Paso, I had caught rubella, then became pregnant with my son, John. I didn't tell my parents until he was born, so they were quite surprised to learn that they had another grandson. John's third son, Peter, was born the following September, while they were in Japan. This made three grandsons and one granddaughter for them.

This was the winter of 1966. They knew they were going to be moving to Weatherford that spring, so Daddy wrote and asked us, both Anna and me, to come home and spend that last Christmas in our old home. Anna came down to Manhattan, Kansas, on a bus, and I met her there. We drove to Albuquerque during a heavy snowstorm. The only time we had any trouble was in the towns, but on the open road, the wind was blowing, but the roads were clear. We made it with no trouble.

It was while we were there that Aunt Mary discovered that Johnny, my son, was deaf. He was a very small child for his age. We managed to get him in to see a pediatrician, and he had the first good exam he had ever had. The letter that he sent back to our family doctor started, "When I first saw the statistics on this child, I thought he had been badly neglected. But after watching the interaction between him and his mother, I realized that this was not true." At ten months of age, he weighed ten pounds and was still wearing size six-month baby clothes that were very large on him. The doctor found that Johnny's heart murmur was severe, that he was deaf and had other malformations. He sent us to have his hearing tested at the Lovelace Clinic, and they diagnosed his hearing loss as profound. The result of all of this was that we were sent to the University of Kansas Medical Center later the next year for a complete workup.

THE WEATHERFORD YEARS

Mother and Daddy began moving that spring. They took everything in the pickup, making several trips. Things went well until they moved the freezer. Each time, as they left the building in Weatherford, Daddy cut off the electricity at the main. This time, he did again, forgetting that the freezer would need power to keep working. They were gone for about two weeks, and when they opened the door, they found a real mess. Mother said it took her several days to clean it up. Since they were moving from a three-bedroom home to an area approximately forty by forty, everything they didn't need for daily living was packed away and stored in the rafters of the metal building. They thought it would be only several months until the house in Albuquerque was sold, but it was several years.

Meanwhile, Granddad had gone to live with his sister, Aunt Rebecca. By this time, she had moved into Ft. Sumner, but she still had her ranch, and he was living out there with her foreman. They were old friends, so they didn't have much trouble for several years.

Daddy made arrangements with a local dairy to haul away their manure and started building up the soil around their place. It was an old, worked-out farm, and it took him several years to grow a really good crop, but he was persistent. He leveled off the land and started planting vegetables. He loved okra and was very proud of his corn crop. (Daddy wanted corn bread twice a day and grew the corn for it.) Before very long, he was supplying most of the neighbors with fresh veggies and loved every minute of it. Mother did a lot of canning, and they bought a big, chest-type freezer in which to store their produce.

Since Mother wasn't old enough to draw her retirement, she started working at the hospital in Weatherford on Saturday and Sunday nights. Even though she hadn't been working as a nurse, she had kept up her license, so all she had to do was have it transferred to Texas. The hospital was very small, and they acknowledged her training as a licensed vocational nurse, so she was content. Of course, she started going to church there in Weatherford and was a member until her death in 2005.

Those were happy and productive years for Mother and Daddy. He enjoyed working with the soil, and she helped him, as needed. They raised almost everything they needed in the way of food, needing only to buy his meat (Mother was a vegetarian) and basic supplies. They also were free to do some traveling, especially when not busy in the garden. Anna was finishing her education at Union Collage, in Lincoln, Nebraska, and I was living in northern Kansas. My marriage had dissolved, due to Johnny's medical problems, so Daddy asked me if I would consider moving to Winfield, in the southern part of Kansas, so they could stop, spend the night with us, then drive on to Lincoln. I agreed, so they came and moved me.

It was also about that time that Anna married Stanley. The wedding was held in Albuquerque, their home church. Mother came and made the dresses for my girls, who were in the wedding. She even made a little suit for Johnny out of a light blue linen material. Stan, who had just gotten out of the Navy, had bought a car, but he wrecked it, (fortunately he wasn't hurt), so they were driving Anna's car, which wasn't in the best shape. Uncle Bill, who was chief mechanic at the Pontiac house in Albuquerque, took her car and refurbished it as a wedding present. After the honeymoon, they were headed to Union College, so I took all the breakable things in the trunk of my car to their apartment in Lincoln.

Shortly after they moved to Weatherford, Daddy was caught in the dispute between Aunt Ruby and Uncle Hubert. As youngsters, they had been very close and that had extended into their adult years. I think that is part of the reason Uncle Hubert retired there. He had worked for Shell Oil Company for many years in California, but when he retired, he moved back to Weatherford. Aunt Ruby lived in Mineral Wells; in fact, she had lived there ever since she had married Uncle Andrew. He was a delivery man for the railroad, taking the packages and freight to the people from the depot.

Just what the trouble between them was I never knew, but they weren't speaking to each other by the time Mother and Daddy moved to Weatherford. I remember hearing Daddy make the comment to someone that he had moved to Texas and was in the middle of two hardheaded people. He tried to bring peace between them, without success. And it was never healed. I do know it was a great sorrow to Daddy. It meant that he was caught in the middle, but he immediately let them both know that he wasn't taking sides.

I think it was in the summer of 1970 that Daddy asked me if I would move down to Weatherford. Granddad had been asked to leave Aunt Rebecca's place, something to do with some antelope, I think. He had been placed in a nursing home, and they were heavily drugging him, and when Uncle Bill discovered that, he asked Mother and Daddy to take him again. When they had moved there, Mother had promised Daddy that they would never have him in their house again, so they asked me if I would move down and let him stay with me. I agreed, so they once again moved me. This time, they had even rented the house for me. One interesting side note was that the house they had rented had a LARGE box of boots on the porch. No two boots were alike. The person who had left them was a salesman for a boot company, so he had only one of every kind. The whole family found boots in the box, but none of them were exactly alike. Daddy had one that was tall and the other was shorter. Of course, under his pants, no one could see it, and he wore them for many years.

It was also about that time that Betty, John's wife, died. They had finished their time in Japan and were sent to Chad, a country in Africa. Unfortunately, there were no real medical facilities there, so when Betty got sick, there was no one who could diagnose her problem. She finally became so ill that the consulate decided to send her to the large military medical facility at Wiesbaden, Germany. Unfortunately, she died on the plane on the way there.

They took her off the airplane in Paris, but they were unable to revive her. When John was notified, he gathered his three children and brought them back to the United States. They stayed with Betty's parents for a time, but that was only temporary. He had applied to have the woman who had been their maid in Japan admitted to the US, but that took time, so he asked Mother to come and help him until Yeno-san could arrive. Of course, she was only too happy to help, so she left immediately. In fact, she stayed for several weeks after Yeno-san arrived to help her adjust to being in America.

One great benefit of moving to Weatherford was the fact that my three girls could now go to church school. The churches at Weatherford and Mineral Wells had gone together and built a school at Garner, a town about halfway between the two towns. It was a two-teacher school, so my two older girls were in the upper room and the youngest in the lower classroom, which meant they had different teachers. The church at Weatherford operated on the "temple plan," which meant that the churches supported the school, and all the children could attend. Each person gave what they were able, and no tuition was charged, which is why my girls could go. There were five families in Weatherford who had children attending: the Rothels, two boys; the Schulesers, two girls; Barbara Wilson, two boys; the Feuillys, two boys; and my three girls. We carpooled to save money since we had to make the trip twice a day, so our cars were really full until Barbara Wilson, who drove a station wagon, agreed to do the driving, and we gave her what we would have paid for gas. It worked out well. I remember one morning as we were on the way, we passed the conference disaster van. The kids all rolled down the windows and yelled at the man driving. I wondered at the time if he understood that it was a group of kids going to an Adventist school. He smiled and waved back to them.

> By the time we moved there, Mother already had a Pathfinder Club started. I think she worked in cooperation with the school. The people still talk about how she taught the children to make bread and earn their cooking honors. They also earned honors on nature, and, of course, she had them memorizing the Bible

By the time we moved there, Mother already had a Pathfinder Club started. I think she worked in cooperation with the school. The people still talk about how she taught the children to make bread and earn their cooking honors. They also earned honors on nature, and, of course, she had them memorizing the Bible.

Daddy continued going to his church, and his brother, Herbert, along with his wife, Aunt Audie, went with him. In that part of Texas, there were several congregations of the Primitive Baptists, so they were often out of town for the weekend. Every fifth Sunday, there was a gathering of the churches that were close together, and Daddy really enjoyed those meetings. Mother made the comment to me, once, that while she always went with him, he refused to visit her church.

Each summer Mother and Daddy had several of the grandchildren with

Mother in about 1975.

them for at least part of the summer, and they really enjoyed that. John remarried and had decided to keep his family in the States until they were older. He had taken a position as a liaison between Japan and the US, so he spent a lot of time traveling back and forth. His new wife, Ellen, lived close to her parents, and he was content with that since it helped her deal with the three children. They soon had another boy, William. Mother enjoyed having them, but Daddy was the one who enjoyed them the most. He loved little children, and they were willing to "help" him in the garden. He was laughing one day as he told the following. He had tried for several years to grow some carrots, but for some reason, they just didn't come up. However, this year, he had a nice stand of carrots. One of the grandsons, I don't remember which, had helped him hoe the weeds in the garden and took the carrots for weeds, and before Daddy could stop him, he had hoed up the entire row. As he put it, "There went my carrot crop." But as I said, he was laughing. He had a small tractor and a little wagon with it, and they enjoyed going places near the house in it.

Both Anna and Stan were going to school at Union College, so when Mother took their son, Jamie, for the summer, it was a real help to them. I remember her talking about potty training him and how much Anna appreciated it when he returned home, and he was finished with diapers.

From the time they had moved there, Daddy, at times, had, what he called, "smothering spells." No one could figure out what was going on until he went into the Veterans' Hospital for some dental work. The day before they were to start on his mouth, two doctors came in and told him that he had an aortic aneurism, and if they didn't repair it, it was a death sentence.

They had scheduled surgery for the next morning. Daddy immediately called Mother, who agreed to drive over there the next morning. She told Daddy that he really needed to let them do it, so he did. It took him several months to recover from it, but it did stop his smothering spells.

It was also about that time that they sold the property in Albuquerque. They had received a notice from the city that something had to be done with the house. It was not in good shape, and it needed to be torn down, so they went back to do it. I think they were staying with Uncle Bill and spending the day working at the property. They had the house completely torn down and were hauling the lumber away when a man stopped by and made them a good offer for the land. They didn't even need to talk it over. Daddy agreed, and they went down the next day, signed the papers, and were free to return to Texas. The man offered to finish clearing up the trash on the land. This gave them the money to build their house.

They had a neighbor, Mr. Toles, who had been a contractor. He helped Daddy do the work. He didn't do the actual contracting, but he told Daddy how to go about it, so they were able to build the house for about half of what it would have cost if they hadn't had him to help. What they had to pay was the cost of the laborers and the material. Mother had picked out the house plans while they were waiting for the property in Albuquerque to be sold, so that was not a problem. Mr. Toles also helped with that. Mother said moving in and unpacking the things that had been in storage was like getting all new things.

When they were finished with the house, there was enough money left over to buy the property across the street—another four acres. One real plus was that it had a pecan tree on it that was a prolific bearer. They gathered many nuts from it and stored them in their freezer. Daddy didn't try to plant anything on that land, but he was very happy that he had it, as it more than doubled the size of their property.

In the early 1970s, I married again and moved to Wichita Falls with my new husband. Mother put Granddad in a nursing home and went to see him every week. He loved it there, since there were many people to talk to, and he got good care. He had a very nice roommate, an elderly man who shared some of Granddad's interests. Granddad especially liked to go outside and walk, and since it wasn't on a busy road, he did it often.

It was while he was out walking that he fell and couldn't get up. He couldn't stand at all, so Mother, after a time, called their doctor and took Granddad to the emergency room to meet him. After examining Granddad, the doctor turned to Mother and told her that in the fall, he had torn all the abdominal muscles from the pelvis bone, and a person can't stand without those muscles. The only solution was to go in, surgically, and retie them. Granddad's response was "Good! Can you do it tomorrow?"

Mother said the doctor told him that he wasn't in any condition to have major surgery. Granddad's answer was, "If you won't do it, I'll find someone that will!"

The doctor looked at Mother with a rather helpless look and said to her, "You go home and clear it with all your family." So, Mother went home and called her brother and sister that evening.

They both said the same thing, "If that's what he wants, let him have it."

So, Mother contacted the doctor and told him to proceed, which he did. He put Granddad in the hospital for about a week to build him up, then he had the surgery. He came through it fine and was doing very well. Mother was really busy during that time because Daddy was in the Mineral Wells Hospital (I don't remember why), and Granddad was in the Weatherford Hospital. She was spending her time traveling between the two of them. She stopped in to see Granddad, and he was telling her that he had walked the hall that morning. She said she hadn't seen him so happy in a long time. She went out of the room to make a phone call, (this was in an old hospital, so there were no phones in the rooms), and when she returned, he was dead. A blood clot had hit his heart. But the whole family said the same thing: he died happy. He was buried there in Weatherford. All his children came to the funeral. I remember his roommate sitting there, with the family after the funeral, saying, "I'm really going to miss him." Granddad was ninety-six at the time of his death. His mind was still clear, and his determination hadn't diminished at all.

He had a small insurance policy that covered the cost of his funeral with enough left over for Mother to get herself an adult sized tricycle. She really enjoyed it. She had always been a great walker, but she could go much farther with the tricycle. She went several times to visit Martha Rothel, who lived about two and a half miles from them, and she did some exploring on some of the roads with which she was unfamiliar. All in all, she really enjoyed it.

John and Ellen returned to the States and stopped off to spend some time with Mother and Daddy. I came down with my family to see them. We had a very pleasant visit, but when they were about to leave for Virginia, John overheard Ellen telling William, their oldest son, how things were going to be different when they reached home. John was aware of the antipathy Ellen had for Peter, his second son, so he asked Mother and Daddy if Peter could stay with them. Daddy was wildly enthusiastic; Mother was a little more reserved, but they agreed to keep him. When Ken, the oldest son, heard that Peter was staying with Mother and Daddy, he refused to go to Virginia with them and insisted on staying in Weatherford. He was in his senior year of high school and stayed only that school year, then he went to Lubbock to attend the university there. Peter stayed with them from then on. Poor Mother was again caught in the middle of conflict. Daddy blamed everything that went wrong on Peter, even when he had nothing to do with it, but this was still better than what he had endured under Ellen. At least he wasn't physically abused.

When it came time for John to go on his next assignment, this time to Brazil, Ellen refused to go with him, and it ended up with them divorcing.

Mother and Daddy in 1979.

He tried to get the custody of the children, the two youngest sons, as the others were not part of the contention, but the courts gave custody to Ellen, and from that time on, he saw very little of them.

It was shortly after this that Daddy's health started to really deteriorate. He had smoked most of his life and he developed COPD, which made it difficult for him to work as he had and still wanted to do. He still tried to raise a large garden, but Mother and Peter were doing most of the work by this time.

Shortly after they moved to Weatherford, they joined the National Association of Retired Federal Employees (NARFE) club, and both of them really enjoyed it. This is a club of former federal employees, and the members were very supportive to both Mother and Daddy. However, as Daddy's strength decreased, there were times that he wasn't able to go. Even after he was pretty much confined to home, they kept up their membership in the club and went when they could. When the club members read the notice of Daddy's death in the newspaper, one of the members came to the house and helped Mother with the necessary paperwork to have Daddy's retirement sent to her, which was a tremendous help.

In 1980, I moved to Amarillo, Texas and managed to earn my associate degree in nursing. Meanwhile, Anna and Stanley were at Rusk. They were working at the state hospital for the criminally insane. Stanley has a master's in psychology, and Anna worked in the personnel department.

It was about this time, also, I think, that Mother had, what I think, was a transient ischemic attack. She said that she was cleaning the bathroom, and then she didn't remember anything more for several hours. Daddy came in from outside and found her completely disoriented. He immediately called Anna, who was living at Rusk, Texas, and me, who was living in Wichita Falls, and we both dropped everything and went there as fast as possible. She recovered and wasn't hospitalized, and as far as I know, she never had another episode like that, but it certainly frightened all of us.

By the time I moved to Austin in 1984, Daddy was really weak. He still tried to work outside, but he couldn't do much. He still planted his corn for his corn bread and raised sweet potatoes and tomatoes, but most of the work was done by Peter, and it really bothered Daddy. He didn't grow old gracefully, as the saying goes. Mother was tied down most of the time, taking care of him. She still managed to go to church and prayer meeting because Peter was there. By this time, it wasn't safe to leave Daddy alone for any length of time. His mind was still good, but he insisted on trying to do too much and would come in completely exhausted.

They had their fiftieth wedding anniversary that year. They were married on Mother's birthday, May 31, but since some of the grandchildren were graduating from high school around that time, we decided to wait until June to have the actual party. John was stationed in Panama, so he came to the States for it. In fact, all the family gathered, and it was a wonderful time for us all. Aunt Mary, Uncle Bill, and Aunt Monnie were able to come, too, which added to the enjoyment for Mother.

They repeated their marriage vows, and Mother sang to Daddy, "Believe Me, If All Those Endearing Young Charms," and it was very touching. We had it at the convention center in Weatherford, and it was well attended. Since they belonged to two different churches, both ministers participated.

We had a meal for everyone. My roommate from Austin, who was a gourmet cook, planned the meal, and we did all the work ourselves,

Mother and Daddy at their 50th wedding anniversary celebration.

including baking the cake. Mother had made Daddy what she called a leisure suit, and I took her into Ft. Worth and got her a beautiful dress. Stanley, Anna's husband, took very good pictures of the ceremony and the reception afterward.

In watching Daddy, I realized how weak he was. I remember making the statement to John that he wouldn't last another year. John scoffed at me, but he died the following February. I really believe he wouldn't have lived out the preceding winter, but he knew we were planning on having that party for them, and he was determined to live that long.

Austin is about a four-hour drive from Weatherford, but I was making the trip frequently to help Mother, so I was aware how sick Daddy was.

Mother and Daddy with their three children (L to R) Georgia, John, and Anna.

By this time, Anna and Stanley had moved to Amarillo, so they weren't as close. John was in the embassy in Panama.

Mother called me one Monday morning in February and told me that Daddy had passed away the preceding night. He had been admitted to the hospital on Sabbath morning, and she had spent both Sabbath and Sunday with him. She thought he was doing somewhat better Sunday evening, but she had only been home a short time when the nurse at the hospital called her and told her Daddy was worse, and she should come back. Peter was there and drove her back. She said as soon as she arrived on the floor, she could hear him breathing. It was only a short time until he passed away. I got my son, and we drove up immediately. It wasn't long until Anna and Stanley arrived. John flew in from Panama, and the grandchildren gathered. My clearest memory of Mother at that time is watching her standing by the casket, looking at him and her saying, "This is really goodbye."

The one thing that was brought to our attention was that since Daddy had been so sick, he hadn't taken the usual care of the car, and the block had frozen. Therefore, it was leaking. After the funeral, John stayed for several days, and one thing he did was to get Mother a new car. Of course, Peter stayed on with Mother, so she wasn't alone, and we were all happy about that.

THE LONELY YEARS

For the first time in several years, Mother wasn't tied down with taking care of Daddy, and I felt she needed a vacation, so that fall, I took two weeks off, and we went traveling. We drove up to Canada, stopping on the way to visit where I had lived in Kansas and stopping at De Smet, South Dakota, to see where Laura Ingalls Wilder had lived as a girl. She really enjoyed that, since she had read all of the *Little House* books.

> *For the first time in several years, Mother wasn't tied down with taking care of Daddy, and I felt she needed a vacation, so that fall, I took two weeks off, and we went traveling*

We went to Winnipeg and spent several days there, among other things, we went to the Royal Canadian Mint there and saw some of the Olympic medals. We visited the zoo and got to see a wolverine. Mother and I had both read about them but had never seen one. They really are ferocious looking animals. They had an old grist mill there, and a place that had never been plowed, so the grass that grew was native. Mother really enjoyed seeing all of that.

From there, we went to see the International Peace Garden on the border between Canada and North Dakota. We spent Sabbath in Bismarck, North Dakota, then drove to Rapid City to view Mt. Rushmore. While we were there, we also went to see the Crazy Horse monument and ended the day at Jewel Cave. Going through Jewel Cave was a real experience. We had been to Carlsbad Cave, but Jewel Cave is quite different. It's all metal stairs, down, up, and down, down, up, and down. There was a platform built at one place with benches along the sides so people could sit and rest a few minutes. Mother was sitting there, trying to catch her breath, while I was fanning her. One of the other women in the group, she looked to be in her thirties, came up to me and said, "You two are a real inspiration to me. I keep thinking, if they can do it, so can I." We were the oldest people in the group, and although we started out at the head of the group, we finished almost at the tail end. However, it was quite enjoyable for both of us.

In the entire trip, that location was the only motel that we stayed in that had us on the second floor. I remember as we were getting out of the car asking Mother if she thought she could make it up the stairs. Her reply was, "Do I have any choice?"

"Well, yes, you can spend the night in the car," was my reply, but she did make it up the stairs without any problems. Before going to bed, she got her heating pad and her tube of Ben-Gay out, thinking she might need them, but when she went to sleep, she didn't awaken until the next morning. That day was easier. We drove to Denver, so she didn't have to do any walking.

While in Denver, we went to see the United States Mint and found it quite different from the one in Winnipeg. For one thing, the mint in Denver was quite old, while the one in Winnipeg was new. The thing she enjoyed the most, though, was visiting the mining towns around Denver. She had been raised in the mining towns and seeing them brought back a lot of memories. We went through the Rocky Mountain National Forest, and she enjoyed that. From there, we went to Colorado Springs and the Royal Gorge.

We ended our trip with a visit with Anna and Stanley in Amarillo. We were there for several days, and among other things, we went to Bryce Canyon. At one point, Stanley asked her what kind of car John had gotten for her. After a moment's thought she said, "A Buick Thunderbird."

I laughed and said, "No, Mother. Buick and Thunderbird don't go together." We both laughed, then Stan turned to me and asked what he had gotten for her. I told him it was a Buick Skylark.

Her response was "Well, I knew it was some kind of a bird." She and I both felt that was the perfect way to end a very enjoyable trip.

I think it was sometime the next year that she received a phone call from John's two sons in Virginia. They had gotten a Cocker Spaniel puppy, and for some reason, they were not able to keep it. They wanted to know if she would keep it for them. She agreed, so it was air freighted to Dallas, and Peter went to get it. It was a large dog. She had thought it was going to be small, and she was somewhat fearful of keeping a large, gangly puppy, but since she had agreed, she would do it.

> *Stanley asked her what kind of car John had gotten for her. After a moment's thought she said, "A Buick Thunderbird." I laughed and said, "No, Mother. Buick and Thunderbird don't go together." We both laughed, then Stan turned to me and asked what he had gotten for her. I told him it was a Buick Skylark. Her response was "Well, I knew it was some kind of a bird."*

Since they didn't have a fence around the property, when the dog went outside, it was on a leash. Being a puppy, and not being leash-trained, it wasn't long until she was pulled off her feet and fell on the concrete porch. She was home alone and couldn't get up. They didn't have cell phones then, so she sat there until Peter came home, about an hour later. He called an ambulance, and she was taken to the hospital where she was diagnosed with a fractured pelvis. (I'm not sure what happened to the dog.) She wasn't admitted to the hospital because there is nothing to be done for a fractured pelvis except to let it heal. It is painful though, and does restrict a person's activities. Peter called Michele, my second daughter who lived in Keene, and she came and got Mother. She was with Michele for about two weeks, then came to stay with me in Austin. Mother was with me for about three weeks, and by that time her pain was much better, so I took her back home.

It was about this time that Marie, my oldest daughter, who was now an adult with kids of her own, decided she wanted to attend college and earn her RN license. She talked with Mother and asked her to spend the next two summers with them. During the school year, Marie's two daughters would be in school, so they wouldn't be alone, but during the summers, there would be no one at home with them. As she put it, "I can only go if you are willing to help me out by staying with the girls." Of course, Mother was willing to do that. Our family had always been in favor of being educated, and this was a chance for Mother to help. That pleased her.

Since Uncle Hubert and Aunt Ruby weren't talking, it fell upon Mother to take care of Aunt Ruby. By this time, she needed a lot of care. Fortunately, she had a neighbor who was willing to watch her and would call Mother when things were needed that she couldn't do. Aunt Ruby had several falls, and it soon became evident that she couldn't live alone any longer. Since she had never had any children, Mother and Aunt Ruby's doctor decided it was time to put her in a nursing home. She was very unhappy there. Mother visited her frequently, about two to three times a week, and since she was in a nursing home in Weatherford, it was very easy to visit her. She said that every time she went into Aunt Ruby's room, the first thing that Aunt Ruby said was that she wanted to go home. Mother promised her that she would bring her home as soon as she was better. "The very minute you are better, I'll come and take you home" were her words to her. Of course, that didn't happen.

Before Daddy had died, Aunt Ruby had made a will, leaving her property to Daddy and Mother, Aunt Audie, and Uncle Hubert. When Aunt Ruby died, Mother thought that her estate would be divided three ways, but she was informed that she would get Daddy's share, while Aunt Audie and Uncle Hubert would each get one fourth. When the property was sold and it came time to settle the estate, Mother insisted that the money should be delivered in three checks. As she told me, despite being married, there was no love between Uncle Hubert and Aunt Audie. Uncle Hubert was a very stingy man and would have taken it all if he had had the chance. When they received the checks, Mother took Aunt Audie to the bank and helped her open an account. As she told me, between her and Daddy, there would have been no problem. They had a joint account, and it was always share and share alike, but that wasn't the case with Uncle Hubert and Aunt Audie.

Another indication of Uncle Hubert's stinginess was his attitude when Aunt Ruby died. She had expressed to Mother, who was taking care of those matters, the desire that her personal things and the furniture be given to the great nieces and nephews. Before Mother knew what was happening, Uncle Hubert went to Aunt Ruby's house and started setting things outside to be sold. Mother wanted to give the TV to the neighbor who had been so good to Aunt Ruby, but before she could do that, he had taken it away. There was quite a confrontation over this, and Uncle Hubert became somewhat abusive. While Mother never started a confrontation, she also didn't run from it. She would not be bullied, and Uncle Hubert was a bully. Renee, my youngest daughter, somehow heard about it and went to his house. She took him outside into his garden and what was said will never be known but to her, but from that time onward, he treated Mother with respect. However, he had nothing more to do with Mother, either. This didn't stop Mother from going to their house. She thought a lot of Aunt Audie and resented the way Uncle Hubert treated her. The household furniture mostly went to Aunt Ida Mae's daughters. She was the half-sister of Daddy, and Aunt Ruby was very fond of them since they lived closer than most of the others, and she saw a great deal of them. She had specified that those girls got special things, and that was one of the things the confrontation was over.

> While Mother never started a confrontation, she also didn't run from it. She would not be bullied

In September of 1988, Margaret, John's only daughter, was married. She asked me to bring Mother and Michele to the wedding, so I did. She had lived most of her life around Arlington, Virginia, so we flew into Dulles International Airport. We arrived on Friday, the wedding was on Sabbath (she isn't an Adventist), and we flew back on Sunday. Since there were so many people there, we were put in a motel, and John met us at the airport and took us there. He also took us to the church for the wedding then to the country club where the reception was held. Neither Michele nor I had been to the Washington, DC, area, so we were very interested in it. John made the statement to us that tourism was one of the big industries there, and they did a very good job of doing it. That may have been part of the reason we decided to play tourist on Sunday. Our plane left late in the afternoon, so we had most of the day to sightsee. What we didn't know and were not told was that the family had plans for the day.

We got up early, packed up, got a taxi, went to the airport, left our luggage, and then went to Arlington Memorial Park. From there, we went to the Smithsonian Institute. That was when I learned that the Institute isn't just one building but a whole series of buildings. We chose to go into the Museum of Natural History and only covered part of one floor. We did see the Hope Diamond. It's behind seven layers of glass. Actually, I was more impressed with the polished piece of topaz that was there. It rained the whole day, and we didn't have an umbrella, so we were more than a little damp when we arrived at the Museum of Natural History. I remember Michele standing at the hand dryer trying to get one of her son's shoes somewhat dry.

When we went to the airport late that afternoon, we were met by a very unhappy group who told us of their plans. My answer was, "Then you should have told us. Since we didn't know, we went sightseeing." Mother had been in the area before, but she hadn't had a chance to do much sightseeing, and she told me that she had enjoyed the day.

Mother in her later years.

Mother and John at the NARFE meeting in 1992.

It was also in 1988, but earlier in the year, that Uncle Bill and Aunt Monnie had their fiftieth wedding anniversary. Mother wanted to attend, so I took off work, and we went to Albuquerque. We had a wonderful time. Among other things, we drove up to Madrid and spent the day there and in Santa Fe. As I mentioned before, Madrid is a "ghost town" and is supported by tourism now. We ate lunch in the restaurant, and while talking to the waitress, who was the owner's daughter, I mentioned that Mother had pictures that she had taken when she was a girl and lived there. She was very interested and asked me if I would send them to her, so she could have copies made of them. When we got back home, I got out Mother's picture albums, took out all the pictures of Madrid, and had them copied. I had four sets of prints made: one for the people in Madrid, one set for Aunt Mary, who had been with us that day, one set for Uncle Bill and Aunt Monnie, and one set for us. I mailed them to Madrid and later was told that they were on display at the restaurant.

Since I lived the closest, being in Austin, I went to see her fairly often. I'd leave my job, at 8:30 or so in the morning, drive up there, and spend the next two days with her. She also came to stay with me at least twice. I remember looking around for interesting places to take her. I was telling the girls I worked with about that and came to work one evening fairly excited to tell them that I had found a place there that I thought we would really enjoy exploring. Amy, our ward clerk asked me where it was. "It's called the Doll House and is on south Congress," I replied.

She started laughing. "Georgia, it's not that kind of doll house," was her answer. It was a "gentlemen's club." We did go to Aquarena Springs in San Marcus and went through the cave at Georgetown. She enjoyed going through the capital building and some of the historic places in Austin.

It was during that time that she sent a quilt that she had down to Georgetown to the historical museum. It was made from her father's baby dresses, probably about the year 1884 or so. She had written to them and asked if they were interested in it, and they were very happy to get it. They sent her a very detailed letter back about her great grandfather, John Ethelbert King, who had come to Texas with Moses Austin. He had settled at a small town named Corn Hill, near the present town of Jarrell, Texas.

I think it was about 1990 that she called me and said that she had booked a week's cruse for the two of us. We were to leave from New

Mother's 85th birthday photo taken in 1994.

Orleans, and we visited Grand Cayman, Cozumel, and Jamaica. I went as her companion, and we did what she wanted, which was to sit on the deck of the boat. We didn't get off at any of the ports. When asked why she wanted to go, she said that she wanted to get on something bigger than a rowboat before she died. We went in the last week of May, and the boat was full of high school seniors taking their senior trip. Most of them were given their father's credit card and told to have a good time. I don't think most of them drew a sober breath after we reached international waters until after we landed back in New Orleans.

It's either the port at Grand Cayman or Cozumel that doesn't have a dock, so the ship anchored away from the island, and the people were ferried to and from in a smaller boat, provided by the Island. Since we arrived there just before noon, Mother and I decided we wanted to watch this happen, so we went to the lounge that overlooked the front of the ship. As we were going, there came an announcement over the loudspeakers that all the chaperones and counselors with the students were to meet in that lounge in ten minutes. Of course, that put an end to our viewing the anchoring.

Since they had a class on crafts that Mother and I were attending, I asked the woman who conducted it what was going on, why they had called all the chaperones and counselors to that meeting. She said that the night before, the kids had really gotten out of hand. They had broken the big, plate, glass door that opened onto the main deck from the bar, and they had thrown a boy off the deck above it into the swimming pool. Fortunately, he landed in the water, but the biggest problem was that one of the kids had taken the life jacket from his room and thrown it overboard. Unbeknownst to him, the life jacket had a device that sent out an alarm when in the water that was picked up by the Coast Guard. They sent out a ship, retrieved the life jacket, brought it back to our ship, and charged the ship for the expenses of the retrieval. The ship immediately transferred the cost to the school since they knew what room the life jacket was from. What they were telling the counselors and chaperones was that if anything more like that happened, the students and the supervisors involved would be flown back home immediately.

Some of the other passengers were complaining of the noise at night, but it didn't bother us. Mother was so deaf without her hearing aids that she couldn't hear them, and while I heard them, I could go back to sleep. They were up all night and slept most of the day. One thing the craft instructor said amazed me. She said the language was so bad that the "air was blue with curse words." Incidentally, after this voyage, the ship changed their policy. From that time on, they weren't allowing more than two senior classes to travel at any one time.

It was also at that time I realized how badly Mother's mind was affected. On the first full day, we went out and found a couple of deck chairs and sat down. We hadn't been there too long when Mother decided she needed to go the restroom. I started to go with her, but she said she could go alone. I sat there for about an hour, afraid to go and really concerned because she hadn't returned. Finally, one of the stewardesses came and asked me if I was "Georgie." When I said I was, she explained that they had found Mother wandering around downstairs, completely confused. She said they had taken her to our cabin. I thanked her, got up, and went to get her. From that time, I never let her go anywhere alone.

It was also on that trip that I realized that a person could sunburn their eyelids. We had taken sunscreen, of course. We both knew that sunlight reflected from the water could cause a sunburn, but I never thought that my eyelids were in danger, but they were since I was doing embroidery and looking down.

I think it was in 1992 that I started working in Marble Falls, taking care of a little girl in her home. She had had a tracheostomy. There were two of us nurses on the case, each one of us worked three twelve-hour shifts, from 7:00 p.m. to 7:00 a.m. I worked Saturday, Sunday, and Monday night; the other nurse worked Tuesday, Wednesday, and Thursdays. The mother had her on Friday night. I would get off work on Tuesday morning, drive up to Weatherford, spend a day or two with Mother, then go spend a day or two with Michele, then drive back and go to work on Saturday night.

It was while doing this that I became aware that Mother wasn't eating right. Since she wasn't having to cook for anyone but herself, she considered it too much trouble, so when she got hungry, she would go get a handful of cookies or potato chips or maybe a bowl of ice cream. In fact, Peter complained to me that she was eating the things he brought home for his lunch. Sometimes she got up and fixed his breakfast, but not always. Since he was young, he almost never got home in the evenings until 9:00 or 10:00 in the evenings, long after she was in bed and asleep, so he wasn't aware of what she was doing or eating. I talked with Martha, her friend from church, and we decided that, with their consent, the different ladies of the church would come and have lunch with her. Since it was to be several different ladies, it wouldn't be a hardship for any one of them and would make sure that

Mother was eating right. The ladies were agreeable, but when Peter heard about it, he refused to let them come. His statement was that they didn't need the help; they had plenty of food. Martha tried to explain to him that it wasn't that, but that she wasn't eating the right kind of food and needed someone to come and eat with her. He still refused, so that ended that.

It was also about this time that Mother gave up driving. Peter had taken her car to the grocery store one evening, and when he came out, the whole side was crushed in. The police officer said it looked to him as if it had been done deliberately. She decided not to have it repaired, and I'm not sure just what happened to the car, but she didn't replace it. There was a bus she could call when she needed to go to the store for groceries, and either Martha or Raydene Epley took her to church and prayer meeting because they both lived close to Mother. She was telling me about one of her excursions. She had the driver let her off at Walmart, purchased what she needed there, then walked up to Kroger's, which was about a half a mile away. When she was finished there, she called, and they sent the bus to take her home.

The driver looked at her and said "This isn't where I left you earlier. How did you get here?"

"I walked," was her reply.

It was also about that time that one day Mother called Michele and asked her if she could come and live with her. Michele said she was crying but wouldn't say why. Unfortunately, Michele's house was full. It was a three-bedroom, and all the bedrooms were upstairs. Michele and Randy, Michele's husband, talked it over and decided that the best plan was to get a travel trailer, park it next to the house, and Mother could live in that and spend her days inside the house. The boys were wildly excited about it. Michele was really looking forward to it, but Marie and Peter contacted John about some concerns, and he stopped it. Unfortunately, Randy found a travel trailer that wasn't in good repair and presented that as a suitable housing for Mother. That was the excuse that was used.

I need to add here that John had moved to Colorado Springs after he retired from the diplomatic service. He had been in Switzerland and loved the mountains, so he decided to retire there. He had lived in Ft. Worth for a short time after his retirement, but the flat country wasn't to his liking, so he had moved.

HER YEARS WITH ME

In 1994, I started working with Pat Sooy, a church member of Marble Falls church. Pat was a close friend of our pastor, and when it was decided that she needed someone to stay with her continuously, our pastor asked me if I would consider it. Since my other job had just ended, I agreed, and I was with her for about eighteen months, until she was laid to rest. About six months before that job ended, Anna went to a meeting at SWAU, and since it wasn't too far from Weatherford, she stayed with Mother. The evening she arrived, Mother changed the sheets on her bed, which was two twin beds pushed together, and Anna said when she threw back the covers, the bed was littered with cookie crumbs and potato chip crumbs, which indicated that Mother had been eating them in bed. We both had noticed that Mother's letters were not in her usual style, so we were both concerned. We met there some time later, and it was decided that, since there was room where I was working with Pat, Mother would come and stay with me. Anna was working full time, and it would be about the same situation as she was facing at home. When it became clear that Mother needed more care, she was asked where she wanted to go. As I said, living with Anna wasn't a real solution, and for some reason, she declined to go live with John.

As soon as possible, I made an appointment with Pat's physician to have Mother examined. I asked him why her mind was deteriorating.

After doing blood work and examining her he said, "She has the alcoholic's syndrome."

My answer was "She can't have! She's never taken a drink in her life!"

He replied, "It's not the alcohol that causes the problem. It's the lack of B vitamins. She hasn't been eating food with them in it."

My next question was, "What can I do about it?" He said that the damage was permanent and that I couldn't stop the deterioration, but I could slow it down with good care. He recommended a liquid vitamin preparation that contained the complete B complex. After doing some research, I started getting a product called "Liquid Health." It kept her alive for another nine years.

When Pat died, Mother told me she wanted to go home. I took her to Weatherford since I didn't have a job or any place to stay until I found another situation. I went to a Shepherd's Rod meeting with a friend, and when that had ended about a week later, I drove to Weatherford. Peter had, during that week, taken Mother down and had her sign all her property over to him. He told me then that, since her mind was so bad, he just couldn't take care of her anymore. I rented a mobile trailer in Joshua, and we moved into it. It was a good thing I did because about a week later, I had to put her in the hospital. Michele and I both thought that she would have died if she hadn't been with me. She was never one to complain, and I really didn't realize just how sick she was.

As soon as she was strong enough, we started walking every morning. About half a mile from our home was a country road, so I drove us down there, parked the car and we went walking, as our place was along the major highway and not a safe place to walk. Each day we walked a little farther, and it was very good for both of us. One thing we both noticed was the trash along the side, so I started gathering it up. I would take a large, black trash bag each day, and I think I filled four or five of them in the short distance we were walking. After I got the initial area clean, I took a small Walmart bag and picked up the trash every day. It's sad how much trash people throw out of their cars.

It was that summer that it became necessary for Michele to put her boys in school. Since she had been homeschooling them, it was necessary for them to be brought up to where their grade should be. Since Mother had been a teacher, she volunteered to take the boys in hand and teach them, which she did. It was amazing how her mind revived during that time. Several times, the older boys would come to me, especially with their math problems, and I couldn't help them. Then Mother would explain to them how to do what was needed to answer the question. Her methods were still intact, and she obviously enjoyed having them there and her being able to help them. When school started that fall, I agreed to go into Ft. Worth every day to pick up the boys, who were attending the church school there. We both enjoyed that, and Jamie, Anna's son, was teaching there that year, so it was nice to see him.

I think it was about six months later that Aunt Mary decided she wanted to come live with us. Mother and I agreed, so she started getting ready. I talked with Uncle Bill and Aunt Monnie about it, and they were relieved to know that she was going to be "out of their hair," according to Larry, their son. I guess by that time, she had become quite a problem for them as she was to be for me very soon. After she got there, it was very apparent that the place we were staying in wasn't big enough for us and all her boxes of stuff. We located a house in Burleson that had been repossessed; therefore, it was in a lower price bracket and a good buy. We managed to get it but then came moving. Michele and her boys were a great help, and we got it accomplished. Mother and I took the master bedroom, since she wanted to stay in the room with me, and Aunt Mary took the other two bedrooms for herself. It took one room to contain all her boxes of stuff. We had to get new beds for Mother and me. Remember, I had no furniture at this time, and Mother only took her bedroom set that Daddy had made and a few other items, such as the China cabinet and doll hutch he had made. When we went to get the beds, Aunt Mary picked out the bed she wanted, although she had brought a bed with her. We got a table and dining chairs as well as some easy chairs at a place that sold used furniture from hotels and restaurants.

I had never encountered a person so selfish as Aunt Mary and didn't realize this until much later. She really thought that house was for her benefit and was most unhappy with me when I let her know that that house was for Mother, and that she, Aunt Mary, was a guest. Soon after moving in there, I got a job working with a home health agency. They had advertised for an RN who knew sign language, and since I needed to work and could sign, I applied and got the job. I was happy to know that Mother wouldn't be in the house all day by herself since her sister was there, and I thought it would be nice for both of them. However, in about two weeks, Aunt Mary came to me and said, "We need to start looking for a nursing home to put your mother in."

My immediate response was "WHAT?"

"She tells the same stories over and over again, and I can't stand it," was Aunt Mary's response. "After all, I was there, too." That was when I informed Aunt Mary that the house was for Mother's benefit and not hers. I was willing to keep her there, but that was Mother's home, and she came first.

Aunt Mary also started telling me what all needed to be done to the house. She thought we should put a pillar in the middle of the garage, and she wanted someone to come and add more cabinet space in the kitchen immediately. We did replace the carpeting in the bedrooms, at her request, but we didn't in the living room, even though she thought it was necessary. She didn't like the board fence in the back and wanted that replaced with chain-link, but again, I refused. This all made her very unhappy. The climax came when one evening when I came home from work, she met me at the door and insisted that we get Mother out of the house immediately. When I asked why, she said that Mother had attacked her and had almost thrown her to the floor. Her final statement was, "Either she goes, or I do." In my mind there was no question as to who would go, and it wasn't Mother. Of course, I immediately asked Mother what had happened, but she either couldn't or wouldn't tell me anything. I finally came to the conclusion that Mother had found Aunt Mary in our bedroom, going through her dresser drawers. Apparently, Mother had told her to get out and probably gave Aunt Mary a push to get her moving.

However, about that time, I had the house outside painted by friends, Verne and Judy Lawhead, a man and his wife from the church in Austin. Since they were staying with me, we had moved some of the stuff out of the extra bedroom for them. Aunt Mary agreed to stay until I could arrange for her to move into the building where I worked, which contained an assisted living facility.

Before Verne and Judy arrived, I had discussed the situation with Martha. When she became aware of the situation, she advised me to get a tape recorder that was voice activated and put it where Aunt Mary couldn't see it. That way, I would know what was going on during the time I was gone. I did this and discovered that, during the day, Mother was staying in our bedroom with the door locked, and Aunt Mary had the rest of the house to herself. I did not agree with that at all.

When Aunt Mary moved in with us, we agreed that I would buy the food and make the house payment, and she would pay the water and electricity. I paid for the phone and even got a special phone that she wanted, as it had an adjustable volume control on it. When she left, she took it with her. When she moved, she hadn't paid any of the bills, so I had to come up with that money as well as the $500 I agreed to pay monthly until she could get the Medicaid started that would supplement her rent.

I made arrangements for her to move into Heritage Square, the assisted living facility, and we got her and all her boxes moved in. She decided to take the bed she had brought with her because she said it was more comfortable, so we did have an extra bed at our home, which made it nice for our new guest room. I went up to her room to see her frequently, but I was working and didn't have the time to spend with her that she wanted, so she soon felt neglected. I'm not sure how she got Marie involved, but Marie and her husband came and moved her into another facility one weekend because she told them I was trying to kill her, and that I was trying to get all her money. I soon discovered where she was because I was in the facility seeing another patient when I saw her. I stayed in the room until she was out of sight, but some time when I was there, she saw me and jumped to the conclusion I was there to "get her." She then moved to Denver, again with the help of Marie. She said she had friends there who would help her. She was with them a short time, then they ended up putting her in a mental hospital. The hospital personnel contacted John, and he was told that she had told them that she had a nephew who would do anything for her. He went to her apartment and began cleaning it out. She had taken all her boxes of stuff with her, and one of the jobs he had was to go through all that stuff and discard what was just junk. He said when he finished it was two or three small boxes, reduced from eighteen or so boxes. He put her in a nursing home, where she stayed until she passed away.

It was about this time that Mother said that she wanted to start attending the NARFE meetings again. We went every month, and she enjoyed them, and so did I. They were very interesting, and we learned a lot about the federal government while there. One interesting thing that happened somehow was that I got started taking the minutes for the meetings, and when the next election came about, they asked me if I would take the position permanently. Since I have never worked for the federal government, I couldn't join the club, but they voted Mother in, and I did the work. I enjoyed it and continued doing it until after Mother died.

In the year 2000, our pastor told us that he had agreed to go to Romania to hold a series of evangelistic meetings. The trip would also include a trip to Egypt and the Holy Land, and he asked if any of us wanted to go with him. I was working in Dallas, taking care of a woman with ALS, but I decided I wanted to go, if I could find someone to stay with Mother. When I talked with Pastor Joe about it, he said, "Bring your mother with us. I'm taking my mother." So, I did. When I expressed a desire to include Petra, he agreed to include it also. The group that went was Pastor Joe and his mother, Zelda, Mike and Terry Dunahoo with their daughter, Michelle, and son, Jay, Christina (Chris) Van Kirk, Stephen Trujillo, Mother, and me.

We left Dallas Fort Worth airport at noon on a Wednesday and flew to Brussels. We were joined there by two ladies from the E. G. White estate, who were going for a time, but they didn't stay the whole time. From there we flew to Bucharest, Romania, arriving there about 6:00 p.m. on Thursday evening. It was then that we discovered that our luggage wasn't with us. The company gave each of us a package containing the essentials until our luggage arrived, which it did on Saturday evening. We were met by two vans that transported us to the tiny town where we were to have the meetings, a trip that took all night since it was near the border of Ukraine. It was while we were in the vans that Mother became impatient. She kept telling me that she wanted to go home. I tried to tell her that we were far away from home, but she couldn't understand that. Finally, she said, in a very loud, stern voice, "Listen here, young man! You stop this car and let Georgie drive. She can get me home!" Of course, the whole group burst out laughing, and that didn't soothe her. However, she had no more to say. We arrived about 5:00 a.m. and were taken to the guest house that had been rented for us. That was Friday morning. We had been traveling since Wednesday, and while we were about eight hours ahead, it was still a long trip for all of us.

Since we had no clothing, it was decided that we needed to go into Suceava to see if we could find some clothes. Pastor Joe had to preach that evening and had no suit, and the others also wanted to get another change of clothing. Before we left, I had packed an extra dress apiece for Mother and me in our carry-on luggage, but we had nothing to wear for Sabbath. That was when I discovered that Romania did not have clothes in the plus sizes. All the others were able to get something, but there was nothing that would fit me. However, one of the ladies who had joined us was from India and had a sari which she put on me for Sabbath. In case you are wondering, they are very comfortable.

It was while we were in Suceava that I fell down and injured my right knee. It was just a skinned place, but it did leave a big bruise. More about that later.

The town we were in was very small. It was possible to walk from one side to the other in about forty-five minutes. There was as Adventist church there, and the people were very gracious to us. They provided our meals daily. We were there over two weekends. Our interpreter was named Vince and his wife was Verica. One of the other people who was there was a seventeen-yearold girl named Rodica, who lived with the pastor. When she was told that we were coming, she decided to learn English, and in those six weeks, she learned enough to be a fair interpreter. We all had a great admiration for her, and after we returned to the United States, I tried to bring her to the USA to help her with her education. It didn't work out, but she told me later that it was my interest in her that inspired her to go to Bucharest and get a college degree.

I went along as a medical assistant, and I measured blood sugars and took the blood pressure for anyone who wanted it every evening. I learned later that they were quite impressed with the care that I took of Mother. I would take her into the auditorium, sit her down, and then go to the table where I was doing my "thing." Chris held a meeting for the children, and I participated in that by teaching the children to sing "Jesus Loves Me" in sign language. They really loved it and sang with wild enthusiasm. Very few of the children who attended had Adventist parents. Most were from the village. It was a good outreach, and it was productive, in that it erased some of the prejudice of the older people.

I need to say something about the guest house that had been rented for us. It was very nice and most comfortable. It had three floors. The ground

Our group in Romania outside our guest house. Mother is standing at front right.

floor was the kitchen, dining room, and a very nice living room or parlor with a fireplace. That's where we spent the late evenings, after the meetings were concluded. We were scattered out on the other two floors; Mother and I were in the middle of the second floor. Across from us was the bathroom. It was very nice, but the bathtub was high, coming almost to my shoulders. How anyone got in it, I have no idea because there was no ladder or steps into it. However, on the ground floor, there was a shower. I insisted that Mother take a shower every other day, or so.

She never liked a shower. At our home, the master bedroom had a shower attached, but the hall bathroom had a tub. By that time, since she wasn't able to bathe alone, I would put her in the tub, fill it with water, bathe her, then drain out the water, step into the tub, lift her onto the edge, dry her off, and dress her. However, at the guest house, that wasn't possible, so she had to shower. One of the things the other people talked about later was hearing us.

Mother: "Georgie, I don't want a shower."
Georgie: "Yes, Mother, you need one."
Mother: "But, Georgie, I don't want to take a shower."
Georgie: "Yes, Mother, you need it."

The other thing they talked about after we got home was an incident that happened when Vince took us into one of the towns. Let me preface this by saying that all the women in Romania, at least at that time, were skinny as a lizard. If you remember, I couldn't find anything that would fit me when we went to Suceava. A fat woman was very much prized there since we were so rare. I was walking down the street with Vince and Chris when a car slowed down, and the driver yelled something. Vince started laughing, then he turned to me and asked me if I understood what he had said. Of course, I didn't, so he explained.

"He said, 'Look at that awesome blonde.'" Chis started laughing, as did the others who were walking ahead of us.

My answer was, "I don't have a very high opinion of his eyesight". Pastor Joe asked what I meant. My answer was, "If he can't tell the difference between blonde and gray, he surely can't see very well." But I was known as the "awesome blonde" for the rest of the trip.

It was while we were there that we went to visit the Romani camp. Pastor Joe had a special interest in working with the Romani people. He had lived with them in Europe when he was younger. Their camp was in a valley, and we had to walk down a hill to get to their houses, and it was when we were returning to the cars that I slid on the wet mud and took another tumble.

As I said, the ground was really muddy, and I was literally covered with mud. I also sprained my ankle, but that wasn't what worried me the most. I was almost afraid to get into the car because I was so muddy. We were going to Vince's house for our meal, and I didn't want to get the car and his home muddy. Vince insisted that I get into the van, so I did, and when we got to his house, Verica insisted on washing the mud off my legs and feet. When she was doing that, my skirt was lifted, and Pastor Joe saw the large bruise on my leg. He looked at it, then asked me, "Did you get that when you fell in Suceava?" I told him, yes, and from that time on, his attitude toward me was totally different. Until then, he had almost ignored me when I said that my knee was hurting. (The original pain was the result of a bad fall I had had in Austin and eventually caused me to need to have a joint replacement). He was very protective of me from that time on, making sure that I didn't try to do anything that could cause my knee or ankle to flare up.

We didn't spend all our time in the town while there. We also did some sightseeing. One trip was especially nice. Vince took us to a large lake, and we went out on it in a boat. As we were going, he pointed to a very steep mountain that had a cross on the top of it. He said that during the communist reign, the cross was replaced with a star; however, as soon as the communist regime fell, the star was replaced with the cross.

Another time we went to the museum of a very famous Romanian composer who lived close to the town we were staying in. (It was there that we saw the haystack. They are quite different from the way hay is stacked in the United States.) One interesting thing that happened was that there was a large plaque that gave a history of the composer's life. I couldn't read most of it, of course, but I could pick out certain things and found it very interesting. Some of the group was near, so I turned to them and said, "Look, it says here that he spent time with...."

Vince was nearby and said, "I didn't know you could read Romanian."

"I can't", was my reply, "But it says here that he went to Paris and...." He started laughing. Because of the similarity of Romanian to Spanish, I could pick out words and put together enough to understand part of what was printed there.

When we left there, Vince took us to the town where Dracula was born, then on to the castle where he had reigned. Romania is very proud of Dracula, and I'm not sure why. He was known as "The Impaler." His castle is on a cliff, and one of his habits was to throw people off onto sharpened stakes at the bottom of the cliff to kill them. His castle is approached with a road wide enough for about six or eight horsemen abreast to reach the top of the hill. From there, a very steep staircase leads to the first floor of the castle. By this time, Mother was showing her age, so I didn't try to take her into the castle. There was a bench at the bottom of the stairs, so Zelda and Mother stayed there while the rest of us explored the castle.

It has a courtyard, and in the middle of the courtyard is a well that supplies the water for the castle. The only way to the second floor is a small staircase behind the throne. I took one look at it and decided I wasn't going to try that, so I sent my camera up with Stephen, and he took some pictures of the living quarters. My favorite saying is that we have proof that Dracula didn't sleep in a coffin because I have a picture of his bed.

In the walls surrounding the castle were slits, openings that were only wide enough for one person to stand and fire an arrow. The castle was truly impregnable. It had only one approach, which was the steep staircase into the castle and the steep staircase to the upper or living quarters.

We went from there to Bucharest and flew to Cairo, Egypt. Unfortunately, we arrived about midnight, and there were problems with the arrangements. It was almost 2:00 a.m. when we finally got to our hotel, but then there was another delay getting us to our rooms. My main memory of that night is standing in the hotel, waiting to be taken to our room, and Pastor Joe handing me a glass of grape juice. Since I don't like Concord grape juice, I was reluctant to taste it, but he insisted, and it was very good.

The next morning, we got up, had breakfast, then went to the museum. That was fascinating. Most of the things in it were taken from King Tut's tomb. We also went to see one of the pyramids. While there, some of our group went for a camel ride. I would have loved to go but was advised that it would be hard on me with my ankle, and since Mother refused to get out of the bus, I stayed with her. It was while we were in Egypt that one of my favorite pictures of Mother was taken. It shows a little girl looking up at mother with an adoring look on her face, and Mother is looking down at her with such a look of love.

Later that day, we went to see how papyrus was made and went on a boat ride on the Nile, where we ate our last meal of the day. As I said in my diary, the meal wasn't anything to write home about. That evening, we went back to the pyramid and saw a very interesting show by lights on the pyramid, narrated by Omar Sharif, a very famous Hollywood actor who is Egyptian by birth. One other interesting thing was the number of military men present wherever we went. Chris was really nervous the whole time we were there. She, alone of all the group, did not enjoy the time we spent in Egypt.

A favorite picture of mother, taken in Egypt.

The next day we were driven across the desert to Jordan. We crossed the point of Israel, where it touches the Red Sea, then on to Jordan, where Petra is located. Petra is known as "The Rose Red City." It was hidden for many centuries and discovered in the early 1800s. Unfortunately, when the English found it, they thought some of the carvings on the buildings were pots of gold and blasted at them with guns, thus marring them.

That was where we had our second encounter with camels. Petra was a city with dwellings away from the main buildings. As I said, it was hidden for many centuries, and the way to it is through a very steep, rocky, narrow passageway. Neither Mother nor I were able to do that amount of walking, so we rode a "chariot" in. The chariot was just a kind of carriage that was made for two without very much in the way of springs. If I remember correctly, the driver stood on a small platform to the side. After we got into the area, the others went for another camel ride, but Zelda, Mother, and I stayed in the main area. They did have a camel lying on the ground that those of us who were willing could mount. He didn't get up, but we were able to sit on him. Mike took a video of me on the camel that he gave me later. We tried to get Mother to sit on him, but she was having none of that! We left early that afternoon and drove to Tiberias, arriving there after sundown. As we drove into town, we passed a synagogue, and since it was after sundown, some of the little Jewish boys ran after the bus and told us we were breaking the Sabbath.

We spent the day looking over the area. We went to the hill where Jesus spoke the sermon on the mount, as recorded in Matthew 5-7. Then we went on a boat ride across the Sea of Galilee. Since this was the Sabbath, we didn't buy any of the things the boatman had for sale, which was a shame because that was also a means for him to support himself. Getting on the boat wasn't much of a problem but getting off was a big problem for Mother. As the guide explained, they had been in a drought for about nineteen years, and the Sea of Galilee had dropped about ten feet or so, which meant that the walk back to where the bus was to pick us up was almost half a mile from where the shore had been, and the bus was waiting. It was all Mother could do to make it back to the bus. In fact, she wasn't able to walk again on the trip or for several weeks after we got home.

The next day we did some more exploring, we visited Nazareth, Magdala, and Capernaum, and we even included a visit to the beautiful Mount Herman. Because Mother was unable to walk, I spent the day with her in the bus. We did see most things, but we missed out on visiting what they think was Peter's house and some of the things in Nazareth, including the house they say was where Jesus grew up. We ended the day with a visit to Caesarea, where Peter visited Cornelius, and driving down to Jerusalem, beside the Mediterranean. Again, I didn't try to get out of the bus, but I did get some pictures of it and the old buildings that are still standing. We got Mother into the hotel by being carried in a chair up to our room. She didn't sleep well that night. Her legs were really bothering her. I did call Michele and had her make an appointment with Dr. Miller, her physician, for the day after we got home. Since she was comfortable in the hotel room, we left her there while we went exploring the next two days. The people there were very nice and took good care of her while I was out seeing the sights. Since I was still having trouble walking, there were places I didn't try to go, such as the visit to the main part of Jerusalem, so I stayed home with her, but on the last day there, the whole group of us (besides Mother) went to see the Dead Sea. We visited Masada, where the Jews made their last stand after the destruction of Jerusalem in AD 70, and to the place where the Dead Sea Scrolls were found.

We flew home that evening. Going through the airport in Tel Aviv was an interesting experience. They interviewed each person and examined all the luggage. Since Mother was in a wheelchair, she couldn't be scanned as the rest of us were. I thought they were going to strip search her. When I protested, the woman who was doing the examining asked me if I had been with her the whole day before coming to the airport. When I said that I hadn't been, she explained that this was exactly the kind of person the terrorists loved to place a bomb on, by strapping it to their body. When I assured her that it hadn't happened, she asked me how I knew she didn't have one on her. My reply was that I had changed her clothes and dressed her for the trip home and since I had seen her whole body, I knew there was nothing taped to her. They finally let us go. By the way, during the aftermath of 9/11, when some of the people were complaining about the security at the airports in the USA, I laughed at them and told them of our experience in Tel Aviv.

Since she couldn't walk, the airline stewardess put her in a very narrow wheelchair and took her to the seat. I, of course, was right behind her. We got her settled, and we flew to Switzerland, where we changed planes. When we arrived, all the others went on ahead. I stayed back to be with Mother, and when I got to the outside of the plane, they had already placed Mother in a regular sized wheelchair and were taking her to the area where the others were waiting. That left me with all our hand luggage to carry, and it was quite a distance. By the time I got there, I was literally in tears from the pain in my ankle and knee. Pastor Joe took one look at me, called the desk, and told them he had to have another wheelchair. We have a picture of me in my wheelchair, combing Mother's hair in her wheelchair. Since it was about 2:00 a.m., all the others laid down and tried to get some sleep. I also have a picture of that.

After we got home, it was obvious to me that she wasn't going to be able to walk, so I rented a wheelchair for her, and we used it for about a month. Gradually, she regained her ability to walk, but I was very sure that we would never try to take such a long walk again.

It was about this time that Mother stopped reading. Up until this time, reading was her main occupation. Her choice was always something spiritual. She read the Bible every day and usually something from the Spirit of Prophecy, but she just didn't do that after we came back from this trip. However, that didn't mean that she had lost her understanding of what the Bible said. One Sabbath afternoon we were with a group of members who were discussing the Bible. The quotation "not many days hence," as found in Acts 1:5, was in one of the scriptures we read, and one of the people asked what it meant. Before anyone else answered, Mother said, "Before long or not far off." We were all surprised at her answering so quickly.

It was also about this time that another indication of her failing ability was demonstrated and also in what high regard she was held within the community. When we had communion, the ladies retired to the fellowship hall for the ordinance of humility. It had an island where the food was placed when we had a fellowship meal. Mother insisted on washing the feet of one of the dear sisters, but when she was finished, she couldn't rise to her feet, so one of the other ladies and I helped her. The next time we had communion, Martha sat on the island, and we placed the bason of water on a chair, so Mother could wash Martha's feet without kneeling. When I commented on her willingness to do that for Mother, her reply was, "I would do anything for Sister Ivie."

> *The next time we had communion, Martha sat on the island, and we placed the bason of water on a chair, so Mother could wash Martha's feet without kneeling. When I commented on her willingness to do that for Mother, her reply was, "I would do anything for Sister Ivie."*

In the spring of 2002, I started getting my Social Security. I had applied for it when I turned sixty-two, but since I continued to work and earned too much, I had never drawn it. The first year I was paid what I would have gotten if I had been drawing it since I was 62, but in December, I was sent a check for over $5,000 to cover what I should have gotten that year. I took that money and had the carpet removed from the house and laminate flooring put down. It made the house much easier to keep clean, and I never regretted it. Later, it was a real help when Mother had to be confined to a wheelchair. It was much easier to roll on than the carpet would have been.

In July of 2002, William, John's son, was married in Maine. Mother and I, Anna and Joquita, her daughter, flew up to attend the wedding. None of us had been in that part of the country before, so it was a new experience for all of us. Anna and I were interested in seeing some of the landmarks of the early Adventist movement. We saw some of the old houses and did some other exploring. The highlight of the trip for me was the visit to Bar Harbor. We traveled on a catamaran and spent the day there. We saw a lighthouse and some other interesting things, and Mother seemed to really enjoy it. There were two boats that went back to Maine, one about 2:00 p.m. and the other about 6:00 p.m. Anna and Joquita wanted to take the later boat because they wanted to see more of the island, but I knew Mother just wasn't able to do that much walking. So, Mother and I spent the later part of the day waiting in the hotel for the boat. Poor Mother! By the time we got on the boat, she was so tired and confused, she kept trying to pick up the flowers that were part of the carpet. This was another night that she didn't sleep well.

    Martha and I were asked by one of the other churches to participate in the prison ministries, which meant grading the lessons and returning them with a new set and including a short note of encouragement. We also supplied Bibles to those who needed them. I usually got them at Sam's, as they were good Bibles and not overly expensive. I had purchased some but had gotten the wrong kind, so I had to return them. While I was talking to the woman, I wasn't paying much attention to Mother, who was standing, I thought, beside me. When I was finished, she had disappeared. I looked all over the store for her and couldn't see her anywhere. There was a guard there, so I asked him to help and together we searched the store again. I was about ready to start looking in the parking lot when she came walking out of the optic department. She had gotten tired and went in there to sit down.

    Shortly after my losing Mother at Sam's, I also lost her at the house. I had been in the office, working on my computer, and when I went into the living room, she was gone. I looked for her and couldn't find her. I got in the car and drove over the entire neighborhood but couldn't see her anywhere. I was on my way back to the house to call the police, when I saw her, sitting on the porch of one of the houses down the street. She got in the car with me, and we drove home, but I realized then that I couldn't leave her alone

Five generations: (adults L to R) Mother, Georgia, Michele, Mary, with Mary's baby daughter, Meadow, in front.

without some way to lock the front door. The back door was no problem. There was a fence around the backyard, and she could go out there any time she wanted. I called Martha, and she and her husband, Bobby, came, and he put a lock on the screen door at the top where she couldn't reach it.

In 2003, I accepted a job taking care of a quadriplegic from noon to 5:00 p.m. I thought it was safe to leave Mother alone during that time, but I received a phone call one day from the neighbor who lived across the street. She said the police were there. I called my patient's mother, and she came to stay with him until the other nurse came, and I drove home. It seemed that Mother was standing at the door, banging on it and yelling that she couldn't get out. Someone saw her and called the police. When I explained the case to them, and they looked the house over, they concluded that she was safe and not being abused, so nothing was done, but I resigned and stayed home with her from then on. With her retirement and what I was drawing from Social Security, we were not having any real financial problems.

Mother continued to decline. By this time, she was talking very little, and it was obvious that she didn't know who I was, although I was with her constantly. She was also losing strength, couldn't walk very far, and was prone to falling. Fortunately, she was never hurt when she fell, and I was always able to pick her up, but it was an indication of her decreasing strength. She saw her doctor regularly, and he was keeping a very close watch on her to see that she was getting all the care she needed. Both Marie and Michele were frequent visitors and were concerned about Mother's decline. Marie and her daughter, Tara, came several times to evaluate the care she was given.

In the fall of 2004, I got a phone call from Anna. It seems that John had spent the night with her on his way to Ft. Worth. Marie had called him and told him that I wasn't giving Mother good care. She knew that Mother had an appointment with Dr. Japas, and he, with Marie, were going to go with us. Anna was very upset. She had been to see us several times and was more aware than John of the situation there. My answer to her was, "Don't worry, I'll take care of it." We went to see Dr. Japas, and he was very patient with Marie, who was quite insistent that she be shown all his records on Mother. He showed her the lab work and all she asked to see, and he answered her questions patiently. He told them that Mother was getting excellent care, and from all appearances, they left satisfied. The next time I took Mother to see him, he told me that he had known from the time they walked in what was going on. Apparently, this happens frequently. One member of the family decides that there is more that can be done for an elderly family member and tries to see that it's done.

It was shortly after this that we, Dr. Japas and I, decided that it would be a good idea to put Mother on hospice care. She was unable to walk, so she needed a wheelchair and caring for her would be easier if she was in a hospital bed. All these things would be supplied by them.

Just because she couldn't walk didn't mean that we stayed home, though. I would put her in the car, put her wheelchair in the back seat, and away we would go. We continued attending the NARFE meetings, and we never missed a church service or a prayer meeting. We had gotten her a lift chair, so when she was home, she was in that. She had an aide who came regularly to bathe her, and that was a relief for me. One rather amusing incident occurred after she was getting help with her bath and before she got her hospital bed. She slipped off the bed and onto the floor. Since the bed was fairly close to the wall, I couldn't get behind her to lift her up. I called the hospice company to see when the aide was coming, and when I told them what the problem was, they called the police, who arrived promptly. She wasn't hurt at all, not even bruised, but they insisted on seeing her medical power of attorney. When Mother first came to live with me, we had both filled one out, so that was no problem.

Mother continued to lose weight. I didn't realize that this was a part of the dying process. Since I am an RN, apparently the hospice people didn't think I needed educating on this, and it's a shame that no one talked with me about it. I was very distressed when I couldn't get her to eat. I first became aware of her declining interest in food when I stopped on the way to prayer meeting one evening and got us both a blizzard. She had always liked them, but this time she wouldn't even touch it. Marie brought her some yogurt, and she did eat that, so I got several containers of that and would feed her one whenever I could get her to eat it. In discussing it with Dr. Japas, he again assured me that this was normal, and he suggested that I keep her on a vegan diet. I ended up feeding her a lot of baby food, which she would eat.

One of the last times Mother was out of the house was to attend the funeral of Martha. She had been hit head-on by an eighteen-wheeler. She had been conscious when they put her in the helicopter to air flight her to Ft. Worth, but she was dead when she arrived there. Fortunately, Mother wasn't aware of what had happened to Martha, who had been almost like a daughter to her through the years.

By early October 2005, it was apparent that she didn't have much longer to live. I had stopped taking her out. I'd get her up in the morning, put her in her recliner, then change the position every two hours or so, then put her to bed at night. I woke up about every two hours and turned her. I didn't want her skin to break down, and it didn't.

The morning of October 10, when the nurse came to visit her, she told me that Mother would probably not last through the day. Her feet and face were cold, even though the house was warm. She was unresponsive and didn't even respond to painful stimuli. The nurse left but said she would return later, which she did, but only after I called her and told her that Mother was no longer breathing. She came and called the agency to report her death. The police came, but since there was ample evidence of her care, they soon left. I'm not sure who called the mortuary, but they came and took her body to Weatherford, where the funeral was to be held.

When John had been down one time, he had emptied Mother's safety deposit box at the bank and had taken all the papers with him. She had repeatedly told me that her funeral was completely paid for, and John had the papers for that. Jamie, Anna's son, came with me to arrange for her funeral, and the first thing the man there told me was that it was going to cost an additional $5,000. I told him that she had picked out her casket and that her funeral was paid for, then I immediately called John and told him what I had been told. His reply to me was, "Don't you sign anything!" I assured him that I hadn't and wouldn't. We discovered later that she had even paid for the opening of the grave. She had made the arrangements for Granddad's funeral, then about ten years later, when Daddy died, she had seen the raise in the cost of the funerals, so she had paid for hers. All we had to pay for was the flowers to put on her casket. And yes, the owner did apologize to me for the mistake.

Of course, the entire family attended the funeral. Most of the members of the NARFE club attended as did many of the town people. She had lived there since 1967 and was well-known. The funeral was conducted by Pastor Joe Gresham, who had been her pastor for many years. I requested Anna to sing "Lo, What a Glorious Sight Appears," one of the early Advent hymns, since it seemed to so represent her faith in the Lord. She was laid to rest beside Daddy in Mineral Wells, there to await the calling of her forth by Our Lord.

CONCLUSION

Mother seldom jumped to a hasty conclusion. She thought things through, gathered all the information readily available, then made up her mind. Once it was made up, it was very difficult to change it. A good illustration is her studying out the truth of the Sabbath, by looking up all the texts in the book, *The Marked Bible*, before becoming convinced that the seventh day is truly the Sabbath of God. I'm also sure, as she read the *Conflict of the Ages* series, she looked up every text until she realized that Sister White really knew the truth.

Mother was never one to preach or even talk about her faith, but everyone knew that she was a faithful Christian. When asked a question, she gave a concise and clear answer. There is no way of knowing how many people she influenced

> *Mother seldom jumped to a hasty conclusion. She thought things through, gathered all the information readily available, then made up her mind. Once it was made up, it was very difficult to change it. ... was never one to preach or even talk about her faith, but everyone knew that she was a faithful Christian.*

during her life. We are told that a person usually has between six to eight contacts before he or she really become interested in studying the Bible, some more, some less, but that is the average. Only when we get to heaven will we really understand just who is there because of her life.

We had a ladies prayer group which met at 9:00 before church each Sabbath. I remember Martha making the statement one day, about eight months before her death. "Jesus is going to return soon, and not one of us, except possibly Sister Ivie, is ready to meet Him." I watched Martha turn to the Lord. I saw the changes she made by her total submission to the Lord, and when Martha was killed, I saw how the Holy Spirit had worked with her, preparing her for the time of her death.

Until her mind began to be really affected, I never heard Mother say a bad thing about anyone. That kind of talk wasn't in her vocabulary. She truly had nothing to say if it wasn't good. I remember one time asking her when she was telling me about her being punished for something she hadn't done.

"Didn't it make you angry?" I asked.

"No," was her reply. "I figured I was being punished for something I had done and wasn't caught."

I never knew her to hold a grudge. One good example is the lawsuit Aunt Mary brought against her and Daddy over Granddad. She didn't let it affect her relationship with Aunt Mary; she didn't shun her or cut Aunt Mary out of her life. Daddy had nothing more to do with Aunt Mary, but because of Mother's attitude, Aunt Mary was still welcome in their home as evidenced by her being there when Anna and I spent that Christmas there, when we discovered that my son was born deaf. It was Aunt Mary who noticed it.

Several times young people in the church came to her asking about marrying an unbeliever since they knew that Daddy wasn't one. Mother's answer to them was very explicit. She was married before she heard the truth, so God gave her special grace. She told them this also applied to those who were married in the church and then one apostatized. She would quote Amos 3:3, "Can two walk together, except they be agreed?" and 2 Corinthians 6:14, "Be ye not unequally yoked together with unbelievers: for what fellowship hath righteousness with unrighteousness? and what communion hath light with darkness?" She would tell them that to marry a person who didn't believe was disobeying God and could not be blessed by Him. There were at least two times when this advice was heeded, and the young person decided not to become involved with an unbeliever.

One thing has always puzzled me. Mother knew the importance of good nutrition. She had studied it, had raised us children with the knowledge that what we eat is what we are. How did she let herself develop such a poor diet? The saddest thing I have ever experienced was watching Mother, who had been such a good Bible student, who had loved to learn and study, become a person who couldn't even answer a question or know who was around her. The one thing I am sure of is that even in the last days, she loved the Lord and was willing to be led by Him.

Mother had often quoted a poem that meant a lot to her, so I had it put on the paper handed out at the funeral. It was a true picture of her faith.

"What God Hath Promised"
Written by Annie Johnson Flint, 1919

God hath not promised skies always blue,
Flower strewn pathways all our lives through;
God hath not promised sun without rain,
Joy without sorrow, peace without pain.

But God hath promised strength for the day,
Rest for the labor, light for the way,
Grace for the trials, help from above,
Unfailing sympathy, undying love.

TEACH Services, Inc.
PUBLISHING

We invite you to view the complete
selection of titles we publish at:
www.TEACHServices.com

We encourage you to write us
with your thoughts about this,
or any other book we publish at:
info@TEACHServices.com

TEACH Services' titles may be purchased in
bulk quantities for educational, fund-raising,
business, or promotional use.
bulksales@TEACHServices.com

Finally, if you are interested in seeing
your own book in print, please contact us at:
publishing@TEACHServices.com

We are happy to review your manuscript at no charge.

www.ingramcontent.com/pod-product-compliance
Lightning Source LLC
Chambersburg PA
CBHW070541170426
43200CB00011B/2502